CULTURE FIRST

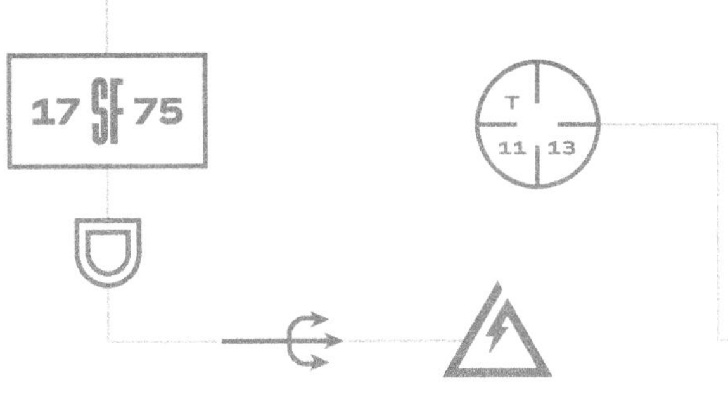

CULTURE FIRST

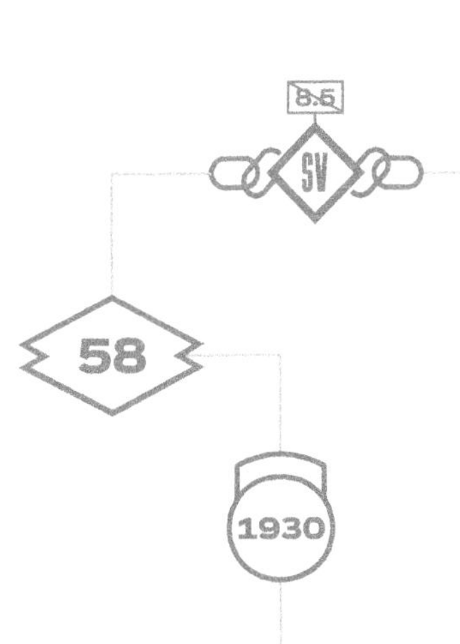

9 LEADERSHIP PRACTICES THAT BUILD ELITE TEAMS

JON B. BECKER

Published by Lessons Learned Publishing

Los Angeles, CA

ISBN 979-8-9943454-3-6 (hardcover)
ISBN 979-8-9943454-1-2 (paperback)
ISBN 979-8-9943454-0-5 (ebook)
ISBN 979-8-9943454-4-3 (audiobook)

Library of Congress Control Number: 2026904427

First Edition: May 2026
Printed in the United States of America

For Melissa,

You are the best thing that ever happened to me.
You are my best friend, the love of my life,
and mother of our amazing children.
I would be nothing without you.

Thank you.

CONTENTS

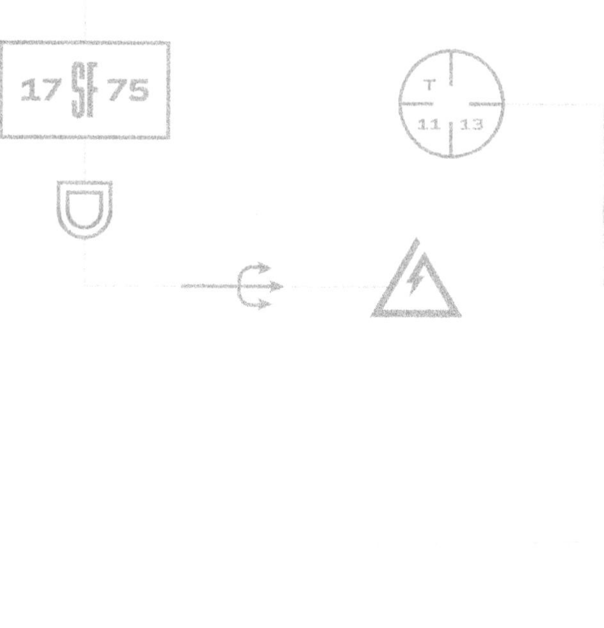

17 SF 75
T
11 13
11 1
75

GD72

SV

41 54

58

1930

INTRODUCTION

Master Sergeant Earl Plumlee was on the floor before he knew what had happened.

One minute he'd been standing in the medical shed, chatting with a buddy. The next, he was face down in debris with his ears ringing and the taste of dust in his mouth. Seven hundred meters away, a massive vehicle bomb had just vaporized sixty meters of the perimeter wall, leaving a gaping hole in Forward Operating Base Ghazni in Afghanistan.

Through sheer luck, Plumlee had been posing for a photo just minutes earlier and had left his gear outside instead of stowing it. Across the camp, soldiers were racing into bunkers following protocol for an attack on the base. What they didn't know was that the insurgents had been testing the base for weeks and had figured out that, when attacked, the protocol was to take cover in the bunkers. Ten insurgents in suicide vests were already sprinting through the breach in the wall, each carrying hand grenades and explosives to turn every bunker into a mass grave.

Plumlee quickly grabbed his gear because he wasn't going to a bunker. He was going insurgent hunting.

He found two teammates in a truck and raced toward the breach. The insurgents were already 200 meters inside the camp. And he saw men in Afghan Army uniforms running the wrong direction and thought: I'll jump out and put them to work. But he realized these were insurgents when they turned on him and opened fire.

Plumlee's sniper rifle jammed on the first round, but by the time his brain registered it, his pistol was already in his hand. He dismounted the truck and charged the insurgents.

The nearest fighter was just seven meters away. In his words he was "close enough to smell him" and close enough to watch his expression change when Plumlee's rounds connected. He worked through the semicircle of insurgents, transitioning from target to target. The fighters shot back and somehow nothing hit Earl Plumlee. But everything that missed him was hitting his teammates in the truck behind him.

"I honestly didn't think I was going to make it that far," Plumlee told me when I interviewed him. "I was just waiting to get hit."

When he reached the far side of the semicircle, pistol nearly empty, he threw his one hand grenade and bought himself seconds to clear the jammed rifle. Then he heard rifle fire behind him. A fighter at a hundred meters was hitting the wall just above his head.

Plumlee dropped to a knee. He knew this distance because it was where they ran wind sprints for physical training. He held on the notch of the throat and squeezed.

The fighter vaporized. The round had struck his suicide vest.

He pushed forward, hunting. The remaining fighters tried to play Whack-A-Mole behind Humvees and containers. Plumlee worked toward the only place he could find cover in the lane, an electrical junction panel, two and a half feet wide. Halfway there, his rifle ran dry.

He started a reload in the open but that's when the nearest fighter slung his rifle and charged, screaming, with his hand going for his suicide vest.

Plumlee's hands completed the reload on autopilot, and he fired until the man's vest detonated. The blast knocked Plumlee onto his back.

His teammate Drew crashed into him from behind. Drew had spent several minutes trapped in the truck by a bullet-disabled child safety lock, climbing over mail and bleeding from shrapnel. They pushed down the lane together, fighting for position behind the junction panel like two brothers sharing a toy. Grenades started falling and exploding in rapid succession. A grenade hit Plumlee in the throat and wedged against his chest. He slapped it away. Another hit his leg. He kicked it aside.

An explosion knocked both of them down. Plumlee tried to raise his weapon but couldn't figure out why his rifle wouldn't shoulder. Then he saw it: a human arm, severed below the elbow, had struck his rifle hard enough to break the stock. One of the bombers had detonated his vest. The arm had come at Plumlee like a missile.

They then found Chief Mark Colbert around the corner, shot through his upper thigh. A soldier from 10th Mountain Division named Michael Ollis had joined the fight by linking up with a Polish officer and pushing toward the sound of gunfire.

Plumlee checked his magazine, one round left.

"Hey, Chief, I can't go first. I only got one bullet. You take point." He paused. "But don't worry. I'll cover you."

They pushed down the lane. The last fighter popped up, tossed two grenades, and yanked his vest. Plumlee ended up back at the junction panel, a grenade rolling to a stop nearby.

When the last fighter fell, he was out of ammo. He pulled his pocketknife and started looking for targets. Then it occurred to him that there were probably more useful ways to spend his time than knife-fighting suicide bombers.

He walked to the dead fighters, found two damaged AK-47s. He stripped the good parts from one and installed them into the other and started loading magazines.

The incoming commander found Plumlee planning to go off-base and attack the remaining Taliban support position.

"Earl, the Poles have tanks here," the commander said. "We'll probably just let them do that."

And just like that the battle for Forward Operating Base Ghazni ended.

Ten insurgents in suicide vests had breached a major coalition base. Their objective had been to massacre hundreds of soldiers sheltering inside bunkers. But a few Americans in a truck got there first and disrupted their plan.

By the time Earl Plumlee ran out of ammunition, ran out of grenades, ran out of weapons entirely and was standing in a field of body parts with a pocket-knife, the attack had been broken. The bunkers had never been touched.

One American, Staff Sergeant Michael Ollis, died shielding a wounded Polish officer from a suicide bomber. One Polish soldier was also killed. Chief Colbert, Matt Horde, and Drew Busick were wounded but survived. Every other soldier on that base went home because a handful of Green Berets bought them the time they needed.

On December 16, 2021, President Joe Biden presented Earl Plumlee with the Medal of Honor, the nation's highest award for valor.

How does a human being perform under pressure the way Earl Plumlee did?

What is it about the way he was trained that gave him the courage to charge suicide bombers with a pistol? The selflessness to shield his teammates? The skill to detonate a suicide vest with a sniper rifle at a hundred meters—and then sustain the composure to joke about it afterward?

The natural assumption is that Plumlee is superhuman. Someone born different from the rest of us.

Although Plumlee is certainly an amazing warrior, the truth is much simpler and more important: Earl Plumlee's performance was a product of his environment. More specifically, it was a product of Charlie Company, 4th Battalion, 1st Special Forces Group (Airborne), and of the United States Army. The training he credits with his survival wasn't just marksmanship drills and combat tactics. It was the accumulation of thousands of decisions made by leaders who built organizations where the right behaviors emerge naturally, where excellence is expected, and where soldiers learn to run toward explosions because that's what their culture demands.

This is a book about that culture and how the right culture can help you to shape your organization and yourself.

What I Observed

At the age of seventeen, I founded a company that equips many of the most elite military and law enforcement tactical units in the world. Our job is protecting tactical operators with everything from body armor and technology to night vision and communications equipment. Now almost four decades later, I have had the privilege of working with thousands of units and observing their practices. Since I was there as the gear supplier, I was functionally invisible. Nobody performs for the guy fitting their body armor or making their night vision work. As a result, I saw how teams actually operated when no one was watching, how they treated each other under pressure, how they responded when things went wrong. I got to know their operators, I went on missions with them, I attended their training events, and I spent time with their leaders. Because of the duration of many of these relationships, I also watched these units go through generations of team members and transitions in leadership.

What I saw was striking. Units with comparable resources and similar training produced wildly different results. Two teams with nearly identical budgets, similar operational tempos, and equivalent access to training performed in completely different ways. One team might perform at a level that took my breath away while the other produced at best competent mediocrity. Same inputs, different outputs. Something else was clearly at work.

That something was culture. The elite units had built cultures intentionally, through deliberate choices about whom they selected, how they trained, what they tolerated, and what they refused to accept. They discussed culture explicitly and held each other accountable to it. The culture wasn't an abstraction. It was a living set of expectations that everyone understood and everyone enforced.

The mediocre units had cultures too. They just hadn't chosen them. Their cultures had emerged accidentally from unchallenged habits and unenforced standards.

The more units I observed, the clearer the patterns became. Elite teams from different countries, different services, different missions, all shared certain practices. A technique that worked for FBI Hostage Rescue Team also appeared at the Los Angeles County Sheriff's Department Special Enforcement Bureau (SEB) in California or at the Directorate of the Special Units of the Federal Police (DSU) in Belgium and at Brigade de Recherche et d'Intervention (BRI) in Paris.

A leadership approach that defined the best SWAT commanders in Los Angeles showed up in military special operations units half a world away. The practices converged because they worked, and they worked because they aligned with how human beings function under stress.

When I applied these principles to my own business, I became convinced they were universal. While an IT product launch might not lead to a failed hostage rescue, a toxic culture will still destroy the lives of the people inside it. The underlying dynamics are often the same. People are people, teams are teams, and leaders are leaders. Simply put, culture is culture.

When I started researching these ideas, I found that what elite teams discovered through hard experience aligned remarkably well with academic research in organizational psychology. While the teams weren't applying scientific frameworks, they had evolved these practices through trial and error. But science validated what they knew instinctively. The convergence between these practices and science gave me confidence that these weren't just practices that worked for tactical teams. They were fundamental principles that transfer to any context where high performance matters.

This book is the result of that journey: decades of observing elite performance in others, years of applying those observations to my own leadership, research into how elite commercial organizations work, and the growing conviction that what works for special operations units also works for any organization serious about performing at the highest level.

Culture as an Operating System

Your organization runs on an operating system you may not have chosen. Every computer has an operating system that determines what software it can run, how it processes information, and what it's capable of achieving. Organizations work the same way. Strategy, process, technology, and talent all run on top of something deeper: culture. And culture, like an operating system, determines what your organization is capable of doing.

An operating system runs in the background, invisible to most users but determining everything they experience. It manages resources, handles conflicts, enables information flow, and determines whether applications either thrive or crash. Culture does all these tasks for organizations. It runs silently beneath your strategies and processes, influencing every outcome.

Most leaders never examine their operating system. They focus on strategy, process, and quarterly results. They hire consultants to optimize their supply chains or redesign org charts. They implement new technologies and launch new product initiatives. But they leave the underlying operating system untouched, assuming it will take care of itself. It doesn't.

Culture happens whether you build it intentionally or not. The only question is whether you'll end up with the culture you want or the one that emerges by accident.

When culture goes unmanaged, what emerges is usually not what anyone intended. A tolerance of cultural violations creates the acceptance of low standards. A pattern of punishing bad news creates a culture of hidden problems. A habit of rewarding sycophancy creates a culture of flattery over truth.

No one decides to build these cultures. They emerge from the countless micro-decisions that leadership makes or avoids making. The defaults take over. Lou Gerstner learned this when he transformed IBM from a company nearly destroyed by its culture into one saved by rebuilding it. As he put it: "Culture isn't just one aspect of the game. It is the game."

Culture is like a reputation: You have one whether you know it or not. The only question is whether you've built it on purpose.

What Culture Actually Is

Culture is not the values painted on your lobby wall. It is not the mission statement in your employee handbook or the inspirational quotes in your quarterly all-hands. Those are aspirations at best, decorations at worst.

Culture is the set of unwritten rules that truly govern behavior when no one is watching. It is how decisions get made, how information flows, how people actually treat each other under pressure. As Daniel Coyle writes in *The Culture Code*, culture is "not something you are. It's something you do."

Think of it this way: Your organization's official policies tell people what they should do. Your culture tells them what they can get away with. And those two actions are rarely the same. While the policy manual may say to report problems immediately, the culture might teach people that raising problems makes you a troublemaker. Although your statement of values may say we embrace innovation, if the culture punishes anyone whose experiment fails, innovation is not your culture. Finally, while the org chart may say that decisions flow through certain channels, the culture might have completely different power structures that everyone understands but that no one openly acknowledges.

You can see culture in small moments. Culture is what people do when no one is looking. And you see it when no one thinks you're looking. When a junior employee spots a problem, do they bring it up or bury it? When someone makes a mistake, do they admit it or hide it? When a decision needs to be made, does everyone wait for the boss or does whoever has the best information step forward? These micro-behaviors, repeated thousands of times across your organization, are your culture. They reveal the actual operating system, regardless of what the org chart says.

The gap between stated values and actual behavior is where organizations fail.

Employees learn the real culture very quickly. They watch what gets rewarded. They watch what gets punished. And they pay close attention to what leadership pretends not to see. Within weeks, a new hire knows the real rules, regardless of what they learned in orientation. Culture transmits itself through observation, imitation, and social reinforcement. It runs in the background, invisible but always present, affecting every interaction.

Why Culture Determines Performance

If culture is the operating system, then performance is what the system produces. The connection is causal, not metaphorical.

What does elite performance require? Talented people bringing their full capability to work, accurate information flowing to decision-makers, problems surfacing early, continuous learning from failures, calculated risks being taken rather than avoided, maintaining standards even when uncomfortable. Every single one of those requirements depends on culture. Talented people don't bring their full capability if they don't feel safe.

Google's Project Aristotle researchers spent two years studying team effectiveness, expecting to find that the best teams had the smartest people. Instead, they found that who was on the team mattered far less than how they worked together. The single most important factor was psychological safety. As lead researcher Julia Rozovsky concluded, "We were dead wrong. Who is on a team matters less than how the team members interact." Even at one of the world's most talent-rich companies, culture determined whether that talent could be deployed.

Culture is not separate from performance. Culture enables or prevents performance. It creates the conditions under which high performance is possible, or it creates conditions that prevent high performance regardless of how talented your people are, how brilliant your strategy is, or how much money you spend.

This is why so many improvement initiatives fail. Leaders implement new processes, new technologies, new strategies, but leave the underlying culture untouched. The new initiatives run on the old operating system, and the old operating system rejects them. Like a body rejecting a transplanted organ, it doesn't matter how good the change is because the culture prevents it from taking hold. Organizations that achieve lasting transformation understand they must change the operating system itself.

The Nine Practices

This book distills those cultural patterns into nine practices. They are practices rather than principles because practices are things you *do*, not just things you believe. You can agree with a principle and do nothing about it. A practice demands you take action.

1. **Build Culture Intentionally.** Elite units don't leave culture to chance. They define it explicitly and hold everyone accountable to it. Culture neglected becomes culture corrupted.

2. **Build a Team of Selfless Leaders.** Your job is to get the right answers, not to have them. Servant leaders own the team losses, and they share credit for the team wins. The best leaders build cathedrals for their community, not monuments to themselves.

3. **Select the Right People.** You can develop skills, but you cannot instill character. The wrong person in the wrong role damages culture in ways that take years to repair. Get selection right and everything else becomes easier.

4. **Embrace Strong People.** The best performers bring independent judgment rather than mere compliance. They challenge assumptions and make their leaders better. The question is whether you have the confidence to surround yourself with people who will challenge you.

5. **Enforce High Standards.** The behavior you ignore is the behavior you endorse. Without accountability, your standards erode, your top performers leave, and the culture drifts toward mediocrity.

6. **Collaborate Deliberately.** Elite teams systematically harvest the best thinking from everyone, regardless of rank or position in the team. Simply put, the best idea wins, regardless of who offered it. These aren't feel-good exercises. They're operational necessities that ensure that teams see reality accurately and maximize the use of the brain power and talent available.

7. **Build a Decision Machine.** Decisions should be made by whoever has the best information and is closest to the problem. Elite units push decision authority down to where the information lives. Waiting for perfect information is itself a decision, usually a bad one. Not deciding is a decision.

8. **Improve Continuously.** Continuous improvement isn't a program. It's a mindset. Elite organizations are constantly focused at an individual and an organization level on improvement.

9. **Take Risks and Embrace Failure.** There is no way to success without risk but elite units manage risk very carefully and always learn from their failures.

These nine practices work together as a system. Each reinforces the others. Implement them together and they compound. Implement them partially and you get partial results.

The Promise

The practices in this book do not require life-or-death stakes or military precision. They apply to any organization that wants to perform at the highest level: to attract and retain exceptional people, to make decisions better than their competitors do, to adapt faster than the environment changes. The principles are simple. Simple does not mean easy.

Simple means the practices are not complicated to understand. Anyone can grasp them. The hard part is *actually doing them*, day after day, when it's inconvenient, when it's uncomfortable, when it would be easier to let standards slide. The hard part is building the discipline to execute consistently over time.

What separates elite organizations isn't that they know something others don't. These practices appear across leadership literature, organizational research, and common sense. What separates elite organizations is that they really do what others only talk about.

Earl Plumlee was a product of a cultural environment where they made thousands of very small yet very good choices. These choices and the practices that they implemented created a very high-performing team with exceptional members who were subsequently tested in the crucible of war.

This is why tactical units are such a great laboratory for culture and for leadership. Every choice they make will ultimately be tested in the most high-risk environments on earth. As my late friend Sid Heal used to say, "Gunfights are pass/fail exercises."

There is no C grade available when people are shooting at each other or on a hostage rescue. Teams must perform at a very high level, under extreme time pressures, with perfect coordination, and even the smallest errors will be brutally exposed. The world is full of people who talk about leadership. But there are very few people who actually lead effectively, especially in high-pressure situations. That is what makes the tactical community such a great source of information on leadership and culture. Their cultures are constantly tested and constantly refined.

You have a culture, your family has a culture, your team has a culture, and your organization has a culture. The question is whether you built that culture intentionally or whether it installed itself through accumulated habits and unenforced standards. The question is whether your culture is an asset that enables elite performance or a liability that prevents it.

Perfect Is the Enemy of Good Enough

The nine practices in this book represent everything I have observed throughout my career working with elite teams. They are the distillation of thousands of conversations, hundreds of training events, and decades of watching what works under pressure.

But here is something important to understand: Not every elite team does all of these practices effectively all the time. In fact, there are probably as many combinations of these practices as there are teams. Some units excel at selection but struggle with collaboration. Others have mastered the debrief but still wrestle with ego. The best teams I have observed are not perfect at everything. They are simply committed to getting better at all of it.

That is why I call these practices, not rules. A practice is something you work at. You will not master all nine on day one. You will not master all nine in year one. But if you commit to practicing them deliberately, you will improve. The mission is not perfection or surrender. The mission is progress.

Use the nine practices as a framework for self-evaluation. Where are you strong? Where are you weak? What needs attention right now? No leader is born knowing how to build culture. We become effective through practice, through trial and error, through the willingness to keep trying even when we fall short. The same is true for teams. No organization has perfect culture. The elite ones become effective by keeping what works, discarding what does not, and never stopping the effort to improve.

Where appropriate, I have included a sidebar called How to Start. These represent actionable steps that you can take today to implement the tool or concept being discussed. These are intended to give you a starting point, not a destination. They are by no means an exhaustive list of ways to implement the concepts of this book. The journey of one thousand miles starts with a single step. These are the first of those steps.

Perfect is the enemy of good enough. Start where you are, use what you have, and try to get better every day.

KEY PRINCIPLES

- Culture is the operating system on which everything else runs.
- Culture happens whether you build it intentionally or not.
- What you tolerate defines your actual culture, regardless of stated values.
- Elite performance requires intentional culture-building across nine interconnected practices.

What Comes Next

Building an intentional culture starts with defining what you stand for. In the next chapter, I explore how elite organizations define their mission, create tribal identity, transmit culture through stories, make values sacred through ritual, and defend what they've built. These form the foundation on which everything else is built.

CHAPTER ONE

BUILD CULTURE INTENTIONALLY

Because the Default Is Toxic

The hallway was thirty feet long and barely wide enough for two men to stand next to each other. On the other side of the door were two terrorists with AK-47s and suicide vests holding hostages.

The lead operator pushed a 180-kilogram ballistic shield made of level IV armor, designed to stop rifle rounds. He had trained with it numerous times. But he had never pushed it toward men who wanted to kill him while explosives hung from their chests.

As the team breached the door, the first terrorist opened fire. Twenty-six rounds from an AK-47 slammed into the shield in rapid succession. The impacts were so violent they would have driven most men backward.

The operator from the Brigade de Recherche et d'Intervention (BRI) kept moving forward.

Then the shield caught an obstacle the building plans had not shown: a small set of steps. The massive shield pitched forward and collapsed. In an instant, the operator was face-to-face with two terrorists, unprotected, at close range. He drew his sidearm and continued advancing while firing. One of the terrorists detonated his suicide vest. The blast rocked the team, but they kept moving forward.

The explosive ordnance disposal (EOD) technician faced his own impossible moment. The first terrorist had detonated his vest, killing himself and wounding the second. But the second vest had not properly detonated, which meant that the vest was still a threat to the team. Worse, he lay in the path between the team and the second terrorist, which meant the team had to step over him to continue their mission.

The EOD technician, wearing only soft body armor (not a bomb suit), made a calculation that defied every instinct for self-preservation. He positioned himself directly over the terrorist's body, straddling the live explosive, and calmly guided each teammate to step through safely.

"As long as you don't touch the vest, there is no risk," he told them. "You can step over him."

One of the operators who stepped past him that night later said simply, "I will remember that forever."

This was the scene in the Bataclan Theatre in Paris, November 13, 2015. Ninety people had already been murdered. The men of the Paris BRI—the police tactical unit for the City of Paris—walked into that corridor knowing the mathematics were brutal: The terrorists had automatic weapons, explosives, and hostages. The assault team had years of training. They had equipment designed for exactly this. And they had each other.

They succeeded when all the odds were stacked against them. Both terrorists were neutralized. The remaining hostages were saved. Of the assault team, only one operator was wounded: shot through the left hand.

What made this possible? Culture.

It was not their superhuman courage, which they certainly displayed. Nor was it special genetics, superior equipment, or exceptional training, though all these qualities were true for BRI. What made it possible was a shared purpose so deeply embedded that these men ran toward their own possible deaths to save total strangers, a bond so strong that an EOD technician would stand over a live bomb in soft armor because his teammates needed a path forward. Values so thoroughly internalized that when the shield collapsed and the plan fell apart, the operator didn't freeze. He improvised, because he understood the mission well enough to adapt without orders.

This is what an effective operational culture looks like. And if you think your organization's culture doesn't matter because you're not facing suicide bombers, you're wrong. The principles that enabled BRI operators to push through this dangerous situation are the same principles that enable teams to push through market disruptions, product failures, organizational crises, and every other moment when the natural instinct is to retreat.

The default state of any organization is to drift into decline. Without deliberate effort, cultures slide toward self-interest, blame-shifting, and risk avoidance. The question isn't whether your organization will have a culture. The question is whether you will build one intentionally or inherit whatever forms in the absence of intention. This chapter is about building it intentionally.

Define Your Mission

A collection of people is not a team until they share a common objective or purpose. This sounds obvious, but most organizations usually get it wrong. They confuse mission statements with missions. They print values on walls and assume people will internalize them. They describe what they do without ever explaining why it matters.

Purpose is the reason your team or organization exists. It is the glue that holds your team together, and it is essential that it is clear to everyone on your team.

Simon Sinek, whose work on organizational leadership has helped shape a generation of leaders, built his entire framework around this idea. His Golden Circle places *why* at the center, surrounded by *how*, and finally *what* on the outside. In his view, most organizations communicate from the outside in. In other words, they tell the world what they do, then how they do it, and maybe, if you're lucky, they'll mumble something about why. But the most effective organizations reverse this. They start with why. They start with purpose.

People don't work for products, services, or quarterly targets. They work for a purpose, and it is essential that we define this purpose not only for our organizations, but for our teams and for ourselves. Why we exist is a fundamental question we all need to answer.

Get that right, and you'll have people who give you everything they've got. You'll have an organization that is focused and aligned as a team. Get it wrong and you have a mess.

When defining purpose, you must consider two essential components.

First, it is essential that the purpose for your organization, and for that matter for your life, be outwardly focused. We are most highly motivated when we are working to help other people. While we tend to see ourselves as selfish creatures, it's simply not true. We will always work harder for others than we will for ourselves.

Second, it is essential that the purpose we work for emotionally resonates with the members of your team. Purpose is something you feel, not something you know. To return to the BRI story, saving the hostages and protecting each other were the "why" that carried those operators into that dangerous situation. Although arresting the suspects and upholding the constitutional values of the country of France were also there, the true why was the emotionally resonant purpose of helping others.

You simply must feel your purpose. And your organization's purpose must always resonate with your team if you really want to achieve high levels of performance.

Of course, not everyone is saving hostages. But that doesn't mean that you cannot have an emotionally resonant and outwardly focused purpose. Whether your objective is making the best cup of coffee for every client, helping people rebuild their lives after an earthquake with homeowners' insurance, or teaching your fifth-grade class English, the mission has to be focused on the people you are helping, not on the money you are making or the awards you may win.

I learned this lesson in the most visceral way possible.

Early in my career, I attended the funeral for Louis Pompei, a police officer in Glendora, California. Louie was off-duty in a grocery store when it was robbed. Because of the crowd, he didn't try to intervene. But when one of the suspects started pistol-whipping a special needs boy, Louie drew his weapon and identified himself as a police officer. He was shot by a second suspect he hadn't seen.

I didn't know Louie personally, but I had deep connections to the surrounding agencies, including my business's hometown agency, Arcadia PD. At the funeral, I sat behind my dear friend Joe Bale, a sergeant who had been one of Louie's best friends. I watched Joe absolutely decompose. Sobbing. Inconsolable.

I walked out with my wife and told her, "This event permanently changed me."

She asked why.

"Because, for the first time, it is clear to me that if I screw up my job, this is what happens."

That was almost thirty years ago. I still feel the weight of that responsibility every time I go to work and walk past the Glendora Police patch that hangs on our wall.

That funeral crystallized our purpose. Not "we sell tactical equipment" (what we do). Not "we provide excellent customer service" (how we do it).

Our purpose became: We protect tactical operators because if we fail, families are destroyed (the WHY).

That's our prime directive. That's a mission worth fighting for. That's a purpose that survives quarterly earnings calls and competitive pressure and all the other noise that drowns out meaning in organizational life.

A very simple test for this is asking yourself: Can I articulate the organization's purpose in a single sentence? I don't mean your corporate mission statement or your strategic objectives or financial goals. I mean your purpose. Why do you exist? If you can't answer that clearly, neither can the members of your team.

It is essential that all the members of your team understand the organizational purpose and that it resonates with them emotionally.

HOW TO START:
THE WHY IN YOUR MISSION

Pull five people from different levels and ask each to write one sentence: "Why does this organization exist?" Compare their answers. If you get five different versions, your mission isn't transmitting.

Create Your Tribe

Once you've defined your purpose, you must create your tribe by intentionally transmitting that common purpose. Many organizations assume culture will spread through osmosis. They hire good people and hope those people will absorb the values somehow. They write policies and expect behavior to follow.

Elite organizations know better. They build deliberate systems of cultural indoctrination.

The word *indoctrination* makes some people uncomfortable. It shouldn't. Every organization indoctrinates its members. The only question is whether you do it intentionally or accidentally. The Marine Corps does it intentionally. So does Disney. The results speak for themselves.

Look at how the Marine Corps transforms raw recruits into Marines. The process culminates in the Crucible: a fifty-four-hour final test where recruits travel forty-eight miles on foot, complete twenty-nine problem-solving exercises across thirty-six stations, survive on just three MREs, and operate on minimal sleep. Each obstacle station bears the name of a Marine hero whose actions exemplify Marine Corps values.

At the end, when recruits complete the Crucible's final nine-mile hike and arrive at the Iwo Jima flag-raising statue, their drill instructors personally present each recruit with the Eagle, Globe, and Anchor emblem. This is the moment when DIs finally call them "Marine" for the first time.

The design is deliberate. The emblem is bestowed by the person who pushed them hardest, creating profound emotional closure. The ceremony occurs at a location of historical significance, connecting the new Marine to generations of predecessors. As Marine Corps doctrine states: "Like knights of legend, Marines are not made, they are transformed. They are forged in the furnace of hardship, tempered by the bonds of shared hazard."

Notice what happens to identity. A soldier doesn't call himself "an Army." An airman doesn't call himself "an Air Force." But when someone finishes boot camp in the Corps, he or she is now a "Marine" (and, note, this title is forever). The title becomes who they are, not just what they do. There is no such thing as a former Marine. The identity persists for life.

But cultural transformation doesn't require thirteen weeks of physical hardship. Disney achieves their desired transformation in just a few days.

Every Disney employee, from parking attendants to executives, must attend "Traditions" on their first day. This orientation, held at Disney University, immerses new Cast Members in company heritage, values, and philosophy. Van France, hired by Disney in March 1955, built the training program that would evolve into Disney University. He designed it to go beyond traditional training. His insight: "What happens backstage will end up onstage. If we aren't friendly with each other, smiling and saying good morning, then we'll have a similar attitude toward our guests."

At the conclusion of Traditions, Mickey Mouse arrives to present each new Cast Member with their official name tag. Many describe this as one of the most emotional moments of their Disney experience. It's the moment they know they're officially part of the organization.

A friend of mine holds a leadership role at Disney. But, unlike most Disney employees, she wasn't really a Disney fan before working there. In fact, she even spent a weekend binge-watching the Disney Channel to prepare for any interview questions about the brand. Despite that, after undergoing their Traditions indoctrination program, she cried when Mickey presented her with her name tag. A nonbeliever, she was moved to tears by a ceremony she would have dismissed weeks earlier as childish. That's the power of intentional cultural transmission.

If you don't build deliberate systems to transmit your culture, random systems will emerge. The same mechanism that can make us belong will guide us to an unhealthy culture if there is nothing better. Your new hires will absorb the norms articulated by their immediate colleagues. Those norms may or may not reflect your values. You'll get culture by accident rather than design.

It is far better to deliberately indoctrinate your team to your common purpose and values and transform them into a tribe.

HOW TO START: INDOCTRINATING YOUR CULTURE

Write down every step a new hire goes through in their first 90 days. Circle the ones that explicitly teach your culture and purpose. If nothing is circled, you're leaving indoctrination to chance.

Tell Your Story

Culture travels through stories. Not mission statements or policy manuals.

Stories are perhaps the single quality that separates humans from other animals. We are hardwired to learn and connect to messages through stories. It's the reason we instinctively share them; it's the reason why movies work, and it's the reason why a multi-million-dollar Super Bowl commercial leaves us talking for days. We are story-driven creatures.

Paul Zak has spent decades looking at the biology of human connection. Through his work on oxytocin (a feel-good brain chemical), he has influenced everything from the movie industry and hit songs to stock trading and military leadership. Dr. Zak's research has demonstrated that having purpose-driven narratives triggers measurable biological responses.

In his experiments, participants who watched character-driven stories showed elevated oxytocin and subsequently changed their behavior. Flat, fact-based presentations caused viewers to tune out. As Dr. Zak puts it, "Stories that are personal and emotionally compelling engage more of the brain, and thus are better remembered than simply stating a set of facts."

Elite organizations don't just tell stories. They build infrastructure for storytelling. Virtually all elite tactical units teach their own history to new members. They tell stories of prior members who were injured or killed and use them to convey to new members what the values and ideals of their organizations are.

Prior members who were removed from the unit are used as cautionary tales. Everyone understands the history and tradition of the unit. The more elite the unit, the more serious they are about their own storytelling. This is not an act of self-absorption or arrogance. In fact, most of the stories would never be told to a public audience. They are the unit lore into which their purpose and values are inextricably woven to ensure they are always front of mind.

This is also true in the corporate world.

Nike created the EKIN position (*Nike* spelled backward): professional storytellers whose job was to spread the gospel of Nike. They also created the Department of Nike Archives, not just a museum but a "storytelling engine."

Southwest Airlines formed a Culture Committee: a "roving band of apostles" who traveled to spread the airline's history and values.

Perhaps the most well-known example comes from Nordstrom. In 1975, Nordstrom acquired stores in Fairbanks, Alaska, from a general merchandise retailer that had sold everything from linens to tires. Nordstrom immediately narrowed the product mix to apparel and shoes.

Shortly after, a young sales associate named Craig Trounce watched an elderly man walk through the doors rolling a pair of used snow tires. The man insisted he had bought the tires at this very location and wanted to return them. Nordstrom had never sold tires. But Trounce faced a decision: Turn the man away with the obvious truth, or find a way to honor what the customer believed to be a legitimate return.

Trounce called a local Firestone dealer to estimate the tires' value (about $25), gave the man his refund, and thanked him for coming in. His manager watched from across the store but never intervened—just kept nodding as Trounce worked through the situation.

Today, tires hang in some Nordstrom stores and break rooms as a reminder. Signs near employee entrances read "Recreate the tire story" and "What's your tire story?" Pete Nordstrom calls it "the best single vehicle to pass on the Nordstrom culture and our service ethic."

Nordstrom's employee handbook famously contained just one rule: Use good judgment in all situations. The tire story operationalizes that principle in a way no policy manual ever could.

Stories add texture to your professed beliefs. They demonstrate your values and provide an easily remembered way to pass on that knowledge to others.

If you want your culture to spread, you need real stories with dramatic tension, characters who face challenges, and outcomes that demonstrate your values in action. Celebrate them, tell them constantly, and through every possible channel.

HOW TO START: TELLING YOUR STORIES

Name the stories that get told repeatedly in your organization: the founding myth, the big win, the cautionary tale. If you can't name at least three, your culture has not been shared through stories.

Make It Sacred

Stories transmit culture. Rituals make it sacred.

Elite tactical units are awash in ritualistic symbology and use their rituals to tell the story of their culture. Challenge coins, unit mottos, mascots, and logos are all steeped in symbolism and rituals that align with the culture and values of the unit they represent.

Within the SEAL teams the golden SEAL Trident is the symbol of their culture and beliefs. Upon completing their training pipeline, candidates receive the Trident at a pinning ceremony, typically from a senior SEAL or close mentor. The SEAL code captures what this symbol means. In pertinent part it reads: "My Trident is a symbol of honor and heritage. Bestowed upon me by the heroes that have gone before, it embodies the trust of those I have sworn to protect. By wearing the Trident I accept the responsibility of my chosen profession and way of life. It is a privilege that I must earn every day."

The New Zealand All Blacks, a rugby team, perform the Haka before every match. To outsiders, it appears to be intimidation, a war dance meant to psyche out opponents. It is far more than that. As James Kerr explains in his book, *Legacy*, Māori believe the Haka draws up tīpuna, our ancestors, from the earth to the soul. It summons them to aid us in our struggle with the sound of *ngunguru*, the low rumble of an earthquake. The ritual transforms fifteen rugby players into something larger: the current link in an unbroken chain connecting past and future. Opposing teams know they are standing before more than fifteen individual players. They are facing a culture, an identity, an ethos, a belief system.

But here's what makes this example instructive for business leaders. By 2005, the All Blacks had lost their connection to the Haka. Players saw it as an empty branding exercise. They were eager to get it over with. The ritual had become rote, disconnected from meaning. Sound familiar? Most organizations have rituals that started with purpose and devolved into obligation.

The All Blacks' response was not to abandon the ritual. It was to renew it. They brought in a Māori cultural expert who helped players from diverse backgrounds, including Fijian, Tongan, and Samoan athletes, connect their own heritage to the team's legacy. The process led to Kapa O Pango, a new Haka that reflected who the team had become while honoring who they had always been. After this renewal, their win rate climbed from 75 percent to 95 percent. The ritual mattered, but only when it meant something.

Ritual and tradition can also provide guidance in difficult times. Johnson & Johnson demonstrated this in 1982 when seven people died after taking Tylenol laced with cyanide. The products had been intentionally tampered with in retail stores by a murderer. J&J bore no legal responsibility. Every financial and legal adviser recommended limited response. A nationwide recall would cost over $100 million and might destroy the brand permanently.

CEO James Burke didn't turn to his advisors. He turned to the Johnson & Johnson Credo, a document written in the 1940s by founder Robert Wood Johnson and carved in stone at company headquarters. Its first line: "We believe our first responsibility is to the patients, doctors and nurses, to mothers and fathers and all others who use our products and services."

The Credo listed responsibilities in order: customers, employees, communities, then stockholders. For Burke, the path was clear. Within hours, J&J issued a nationwide recall of thirty-one million bottles.

"The Credo made it very clear at that point exactly what we were all about," Burke later reflected. Within six months, Tylenol had climbed back to around 30 percent market share. The Credo wasn't just words on stone. It was a decision-making framework when stakes were highest.

Symbols, rituals, and documents become sacred when they're earned through difficulty, bestowed by people who matter, connected to history, and reinforced daily. Elite units use symbols to tell their story. Their challenge coins, team mottos, and unit symbols are all extensions of their story and they reinforce their cultural brand. The same can be seen in elite corporate environments and elite sports teams. What are you ritualizing, and how do the symbols of your organization support your cultural story?

Defend the Village

Culture is not self-sustaining. It requires active defense by the individual, the leaders, and the organization.

Left alone, culture will degrade. It will drift toward self-interest, blame-shifting, and whatever behaviors people can get away with. Every exception that you make, every violation that you tolerate, every bad actor you accommodate erodes the cultural foundation.

When threats to the culture occur, they must be dealt with swiftly and decisively. The greater the threat to the organizational culture, the more robust and public the response needs to be.

As a leader it is essential that you always defend your organization's culture because the things you choose to defend, or more importantly to not defend, tell everyone in the organization what matters. There are few more powerful statements about what you value than terminating someone's role on the team.

In elite units, cultural transgressions are dealt with swiftly, publicly, and clearly. Severe transgressions will result in the person being removed from the unit. One interesting aspect of elite unit culture is that these removals are usually commemorated in some way to clearly indicate unacceptable behavior. For some units the former member is given a persona non grata status where he or she is no longer welcome at the unit's headquarters or on their compound. For others it will result in that person being stricken from the unit's history as if they didn't exist.

At the Los Angeles County Sheriff's Department Special Enforcement Bureau (SEB) each member of the unit is commemorated by a brick with their name on it on the walkway to their unit memorial. Cross the line and get removed from the unit and your brick will be turned upside down to tell everyone you are no longer seen as part of the unit or its history.

The SEALs have perhaps the most visceral ritual. They convene what is called a Trident board, which can strip a SEAL of his Trident. This means what it sounds like: You are no longer a SEAL. But it goes much further. That man is no longer considered to have ever been a SEAL. This is robust, public action to defend the culture.

I learned about the need to defend our values through an experience that left no room for ambiguity in my mind.

We had a forty-five-year-old warehouse employee, a man, who was making a nineteen-year-old female coworker uncomfortable. He had gone to her house uninvited and knocked on her door. He gave her a Valentine's Day card after work one day. He was twenty-five years older than she, and in her words was older than her dad. She didn't want to make waves, but she mentioned it to one of our female directors, and after that the actions spread like wildfire. Sexual harassment is not something our tribe tolerates.

I was at an off-site meeting when this director called me: "You are not gonna believe this shit," she said. "Here is what he did."

This was clearly a moment that was testing our culture and my strength as a leader. "I know exactly what I want to do," I said. "I will handle this."

I called his supervisor, told him what happened and sought his counsel.

"We need to fire him," was the supervisor's reply.

I agreed. "Pull him in, see if he confirms it, and fire him on the spot."

He confirmed it and was unemployed an hour after I learned about it.

The message was very clear: this is not how we treat our teammates. This was not a difficult choice in my brain because I have strong beliefs about my role as a leader. More importantly, it was not a difficult choice in our culture.

That said, when news spread of his firing, every female in the organization said, in effect, "Hell yes, they fired him immediately. They care about us."

Sometimes swift and decisive action is necessary, which can be awkward. As the leader you manifest accountability and your culture in both directions. You're the one who undermines the culture by being inconsistent or cowardly. You're also the one who reinforces it by acting decisively when the moment requires it.

The easiest place to protect culture is at the door, which I will talk more about later. But even with rigorous selection, threats will emerge. When they do, your response defines your culture far more than your mission statement ever will.

Always remember that everyone is watching.

HOW TO START:
IDENTIFYING CULTURE THREATS

Identify the three behaviors or attitudes currently eroding your culture. Be specific. For each one, ask yourself, am I addressing this directly, or hoping it resolves itself?

KEY PRINCIPLES

- Define your mission in terms of WHY, not WHAT.
- Create tribal identity through shared hardship and deliberate indoctrination.
- Stories transmit culture; saturate your environment with narratives that demonstrate values in action.
- Rituals make values sacred—but only when connected to meaning.
- Culture must be actively defended; threats that go unchallenged become the new standard.

What Comes Next

Culture is the foundation, but the right culture doesn't emerge by accident. It is built by leaders who model what they want to see, who subordinate their ego to the mission, and who create environments where people can bring their best. Leadership is the variable that determines whether your culture lives or dies. That's where we turn next.

CHAPTER TWO

BUILD A TEAM OF SELFLESS LEADERS

It's Not About You

On January 31, 2025, Brian Driscoll sat in the FBI Director's office on the seventh floor of the J. Edgar Hoover Building and faced a choice that would define his career.

He had been acting director for only eleven days when the acting deputy attorney general ordered him to compile a list of every FBI employee who had worked on January 6 investigations. This would be thousands of names. The purpose was clear. They wanted to perform a "personnel review": a euphemism for mass firings.

Driscoll was an unlikely person to find himself in this position. He had spent eighteen years as an

FBI special agent and had managed to avoid being at headquarters. In fact, some would argue that he had crafted the perfect FBI career. He was a decorated operator on the Hostage Rescue Team, the Bureau's elite tactical unit. He had earned the Medal of Valor for a joint raid with Delta Force in Syria and the Shield of Bravery for neutralizing an active shooter in upstate New York.

He had also been the commander of HRT, the commander of the Critical Incident Response Group, and one week before the inauguration, he had just been promoted to Special Agent In Charge of the Newark field office. He was a rising star in the FBI and was beloved by the people who had worked with him, especially the Hostage Rescue Team.

Then a clerical error on the White House website listed him as acting director instead of his colleague Robert Kissane, and the administration decided not to correct it. Now the accidental director had a decision to make.

He could assemble the list as he was ordered to do and thereby protect his career. He could simply distance himself from the agents being targeted, quietly comply, and then let someone else deal with the consequences. That's what a careful bureaucrat would do, and his career would likely survive.

But Brian Driscoll is not a careful bureaucrat. He is a man of action, and he did not believe what he was being asked to do was legal or ethical. So he refused to provide the requested list and sent a memo to the entire FBI workforce, transparently sharing the directive he had received. In that memo he included a single sentence that transformed him from acting director into something closer to a folk hero: "I am one of those employees, as is Acting Deputy Director Kissane."

With those first six words, Driscoll demonstrated what servant leadership looks like under fire. He did not ask his people to face consequences he was unwilling to face himself. He made it impossible for anyone to claim this was about individual misconduct and stepped directly into the fire on behalf of his agents. And he communicated to thousands of frightened agents that their leader was standing with them, not above them.

The response was immediate. Within days, FBI agents were sharing memes depicting Driscoll as a saint, as Batman fighting bureaucratic villains. "What Would Driz Do?" became an internal rallying cry. The FBI Agents Association later noted that he "courageously stood shoulder-to-shoulder with the men and women in the field."

As a result of his actions, the apparently planned mass layoffs did not occur and the moment passed leaving all of those agents in their jobs and, more importantly, not gutting the FBI and damaging its operational capability.

Six months later, Driscoll was fired. His termination letter cited no misconduct, offered no due process, provided no explanation.

In his farewell message to colleagues, he wrote: "Last night I was informed that tomorrow will be my last day in the FBI. I understand that you may have a lot of questions regarding why, for which I currently have no answers. No cause has been articulated at this time. Please know that it has been the honor of my life to serve alongside each of you. Our collective sacrifices for those we serve is, and will always be, worth it. I regret nothing. You are my heroes and I remain in your debt."

"I regret nothing."

That is selfless leadership. It is placing the needs of the organization above the needs of the leader and ensuring that the organization is as effective as it can be.

Your job as a leader seems simple—just get 100 percent out of all the resources available to you. Every person on your team has capabilities, ideas, energy, and commitment that you need to access. Leadership is the discipline of nurturing those people and their capabilities. It is about building an environment and structures that maximize what your people can contribute.

But that does not emerge in a vacuum; effective teams are cultivated by leaders who model that selflessness. They are protected by leaders who stand with them when things get hard. They are inspired by leaders who demonstrate, through their actions, that rank imposes responsibility, not privilege.

Leaders Are Built, Not Born

There is a notion that good leaders are somehow born that way; that we either have the gift or we don't. Yet nothing could be further from the truth. Leadership is a series of behaviors, not an innate ability.

Early in my career my friend Sid Heal told me that "nobody is born a leader. The capacity to lead is forged through failure, training, hardship, and experience."

Every effective leader I have encountered earned that capability the hard way. They made mistakes. They learned. They made different mistakes. They learned again. The process never ends.

Being a good leader means working at it. It means trying things, failing, apologizing for your failures, then getting better educated, and trying new things.

The first step to being an effective leader is to realize that leadership emerges from an intentional process.

In forty years of leading people, I have made just about every mistake there is to make. I have hired the wrong people, fired the wrong people, said the wrong things, stayed silent when I should have spoken, and spoken when I should have stayed silent. Every day I try not to make new mistakes. Some days I succeed. Some days I do not.

As a leader, you are the cultural icon for your team. Your behavior sets the standard. Your reactions define what is acceptable. Your priorities become their priorities. This is an enormous responsibility, but it is also an enormous opportunity. Every day, through your actions, you get to show your people what this organization values and who we aspire to be.

You must always manifest the highest form of what you want to see in your team. If you want honesty, you must be the most honest person in the room. If you want humility, you must be the first to admit when you are wrong. If you want people who care deeply about the mission and each other, you must care more deeply than anyone. You must clearly own failures, laugh at your own imperfections, and remain on a perpetual quest to do a better job tomorrow than you did today.

The best leaders I know live in quiet fear of harming their people or letting them down. This is not a weakness, it is exactly the right mindset. That fear keeps you vigilant. It keeps you honest. It keeps you working to be worthy of the responsibility you have been given.

You do not have to be perfect. It is acceptable to show weakness. You are always a work in progress, and the people you lead know it. The more authentic you are about your own struggles and limitations, the greater trust you will build with your team. Pretending to have all the answers fools no one and creates distance between you and the people who need to trust you most.

The Roman Stoic philosopher Seneca captured this spirit of continuous self-improvement in his moral letters: "It is enough for me if every day I reduce the number of my vices and blame my mistakes." That is the standard. Not perfection. Progress.

HOW TO START: BUILDING A BETTER YOU

What are you doing to improve your leadership and develop other leaders in your organization? If you are not intentionally building a better you, it is not happening!

Ego Is the Enemy

The first step down this road is humility. Humility is the root of effective leadership as well as the foundation for harvesting the capabilities of your team.

Ego, arrogance, and hubris are a lethal combination for tactical units. Ego creates blind spots. It prevents learning, breeds overconfidence, and ultimately leads to fatal mistakes.

Virtually all elite units select specifically for people who are humble. They want people who are highly capable but balance that capability with a healthy dose of humility.

This doesn't mean they aren't confident. But confidence and ego are not the same. Confidence is faith in your abilities. Ego is a belief in your own superiority. Ego is dangerous in tactical units as well as in the corporate world.

Throughout my career I have noticed one paradoxical quality about ego: The teams that are not that good are usually the most egotistical. They have the most swagger, the loudest war stories, the greatest certainty about their own excellence.

The truly elite teams are different. They're humble. They're hungry. They assume there's always more to learn, always someone doing it better, always a way to improve.

You can't learn if you're not humble. And you can't be humble if your ego is running the show. It is essential in building any organization that ego and arrogance are not allowed to thrive.

This is true for every member of your team, but it is absolutely essential for the leaders in the organization. Humble leadership is the foundation for excellence and your ability to model this behavior will underlie most of the cultural practices that follow. It is not about you.

HOW TO START: CHECKING YOUR EGO

Think about the last time someone disagreed with you. Did you listen to them to understand what they were saying or just to respond? If you don't try to understand others, you don't provide safety for honest answers.

Leaders Eat Last

If you visit a US Marine Corps mess hall, you will notice something unusual. The most senior person always eats last. This tradition is not a symbolic gesture or performed for effect or appearances. It is rooted in Marine doctrine, practiced at every meal, in every mess hall, throughout the organization.

Simon Sinek, who discussed this observation in his book *Leaders Eat Last*, describes watching the most junior Marine go through the line first while senior officers stood by. The message it sends is unmistakable, the needs of your people always come before your own.

This is an example of a broader philosophy that lies at the core of elite tactical units. Leaders exist to provide resources and support to those they lead. Your people are more important than you are.

If being a good teammate means being concerned about the person to your left and right, then being a good leader means caring more about those you lead than you do about yourself.

The ancient Chinese general Sun Tzu captured it succinctly: "Regard your soldiers as your children, and they will follow you into the deepest valleys. Look on them as your own beloved sons, and they will stand by you even unto death." People perform at their highest level when they know their leader genuinely cares about their welfare.

Lee McMillion, the commander of LAPD D-Platoon (aka SWAT), sees his role this way: "Selflessness. I think that if you're selfless, your team knows that you are there for them." His mantra also applies here, "Take care of the man next to you better than yourself." It's what teammates owe each other, but it's also what leaders owe to their teams.

The skeptic might dismiss this as military romanticism, inapplicable to business settings where lives are not on the line. But Toyota has codified the same philosophy into their management system. The Toyota Way rests on two pillars: continuous improvement and respect for people. That second pillar is not a feel-good slogan; it is a behavioral expectation that lies at the heart of all decisions, problem-solving, and daily interactions.

At Toyota, respect means caring about people. Leaders are expected to develop their people, not just manage them. This shows up in cultural practices like *genchi genbutsu* (literally, "go and see"), where leaders are taught to be on the shop floor with their teams, not in offices. *Genchi genbutsu* expects leaders to observe work where it happens, speak with those closest to the problems, and understand the views of their teams before making decisions.

This is not "be a nice boss" leadership. It is systematic operational leadership focused on those you lead. It reflects a very mature interpretation of servant leadership, which is not altruism, but commitment to people and process over selfishness and ego.

Peter Drucker, the father of modern management, captured this principle in a single line: "Rank does not confer privilege or give power. It imposes responsibility." The higher you climb, the more you owe to those below you. That is the bargain of leadership.

HOW TO START: SERVING YOUR TEAM

When your team has meals, cleans up, or works together what is your role and place? Do you put them in front of you or do you go first? Do you literally eat last?

Find the Path

We have all worked for the leader who has to "have all the answers." This is the one who takes credit for actions he did not do, who has to control everything, who cannot admit uncertainty. When you are a young leader, this feels like strength. You feel pressure to know everything, to have the solution ready, to project confidence at all times. I know, because I've been there.

Perhaps the greatest mistake I made as a young leader was carrying the belief that I had to be the source of answers for every question. I probably felt like being in charge meant I had to be the smartest guy in the room.

Not surprisingly, I often failed to harness all the amazing brain power available to me through employees, clients, advisers, and friends. When you appoint yourself the source of all answers, three things happen: (1) You become the only voice that matters, (2) no one will question your authority or challenge your thinking, and (3) you silence all your available resources.

Steve Jobs reportedly once said, "It doesn't make sense to hire smart people and then tell them what to do. We hire smart people so they can tell us what to do."

The feeling that you are the smartest person in the room is rooted either in ego and arrogance or in insecurity and impostor syndrome. In either case, that feeling will prevent you from effectively leading the team.

Here is a principle I wish I had understood decades earlier: An effective leader is a person who can *find* the right answer to every problem. It is not the one who must *have* the right answer.

This distinction matters a great deal. The "answer-haver" must always appear knowledgeable, falls in love with their own decisions, sees questions as threats to their authority, and surrounds themself with yes-people.

The "pathfinder" is comfortable not knowing, remains open to changing course, sees curiosity as strength, and surrounds themself with people who challenge their thinking and tell them the truth.

In tactical operations, there is no room for the answer-haver's ego. Mistakes cost lives. As a result, tactical leaders learn to rely on their designated experts and seek out contrary views before committing to a course of action.

Mike Hillmann is a legendary LAPD D-Platoon member and National Tactical Officers Association (NTOA) Hall of Honor inductee. Hillmann describes his approach this way: "I always looked at my strengths as being able to bring people together, as being able to listen, and to engage people that were a lot smarter than I was." He adds a critical insight: "Good leaders never fall in love with their own decisions. They always want to listen."

Pete Blaber, a retired Delta Force commander, teaches a simple technique to unlock the tacit knowledge bottled up inside your team. Ask them how they would handle it if they were in charge. That single question transforms a subordinate into a strategic contributor.

Blaber's broader principle is equally powerful: "Always listen to the guy on the ground." He notes that "if you're right 50 percent of the time in your life, that's a pretty good batting average. Tapping into guys on the ground is the way to self-correct." The leader's job is not to be right. It is to *find* right.

Inspector Kevin Cyr, who commands the Royal Canadian Mounted Police Lower Mainland District Integrated Emergency Response Team in British Columbia, takes this principle to its logical conclusion. He once told his team: "Don't ask me questions I don't have situational awareness to answer." Think about that. A senior commander explicitly tells his people that he should not be making certain decisions because he lacks the information to make them well. That requires profound confidence and profound humility simultaneously.

Cyr is also refreshingly honest about the emotional reality of leadership. "I feel the pressure, this weighing pressure that maybe I'm going to make a mistake," he admits. "And it sucks. Maybe I'm a wimp. I don't think so. But I find these things scary."

After one particularly challenging operation, he acknowledged: "I was not experienced enough for that call. My cup was full, for sure." This is an elite tactical commander admitting he was in over his head and demonstrating that vulnerability is not weakness. It is the prerequisite for learning and improvement.

Gary Klein, regarded as the father of decision-making research, explains the correct mindset with a simple phrase: "I don't know. Let's talk about it and see what we can figure out." In other words, you have my permission for everyone else to contribute to my thinking.

Klein notes that the best leaders he has studied share one characteristic: "They are the most curious people I know." Curiosity can feel vulnerable because it suggests you do not know something. But leaders who embrace curiosity consistently arrive at better answers than those who project false certainty.

It is essential that we are always focused on finding the right path no matter where that plan comes from. In our personal lives or in our professional lives, viewing your responsibility as that of a pathfinder opens you up to the ideas of others, allows for constructive disagreement, and also eliminates the need to constantly defend your ideas.

Peter Drucker said perfectly, "The leader of the past was a person who knew how to tell. The leader of the future will be a person who knows how to ask."

> **HOW TO START: BEING A PATHFINDER**
>
> For one day, track every time someone asks you a question. How many times did you give the answer versus ask "What do you think?" If you always provide the answer, you're the bottleneck.

Own the Loss, Share the Win

As a leader it is essential that you take responsibility for things that do not go well. In *Extreme Ownership*, Jocko Willink tells the story of his SEAL unit being engaged in heavy combat in Ramadi, Iraq, in 2006. During one complex nighttime operation, a friendly fire incident killed an Iraqi soldier and wounded several others, including one of Willink's own SEALs. In the chaos of urban combat, multiple errors had compounded. Communication broke down, units moved into each other's areas of operation, and incomplete information was flowing in every direction.

When Willink's commanding officer asked who was responsible for the failed operation, Willink could have easily distributed blame across multiple parties. The Iraqi soldiers had made mistakes, other units had moved into his area unexpectedly, and the fog of war had created conditions no one could fully control.

Instead, Willink said simply, "There is only one person to blame for this: me."

Willink genuinely believed that, as the leader, every failure in his organization was ultimately his responsibility. The inadequate communication, the insufficient coordination, the chaos of the operation all traced back to something he could have done better. What happened next surprised everyone. Rather than ending his career, this act of extreme ownership earned Willink greater trust up and down his chain of command. By taking responsibility without excuses, he demonstrated exactly the kind of leadership the SEALs value most.

Pete Blaber makes an important distinction between responsibility and blame. "There's a big difference between taking responsibility and taking blame," Blaber explains. "When you take responsibility, you're acknowledging that you're responsible and accountable for everything that happens while you're in a position of leadership. Taking blame means you're saying it was my fault, I did it, something I did caused it."

Leaders can take responsibility without accepting blame for things genuinely outside their control. The key is the posture and always asking, "What could I have done differently?" rather than "Whose fault was this?"

The inverse principle applies to successes. When things go well, good leaders instinctively redirect credit outward. "We" dominates their vocabulary. Individual recognition flows to the people who did the work, not the leader who orchestrated it.

Another way to describe this is to "personalize your losses" and "socialize your victories." Take responsibility when you lose or fail. Share all the credit when you win. Your team will trust you more and you will be a more effective leader.

On July 22, 2011, Norway experienced its worst terrorist attack since World War II. A lone attacker detonated a bomb in Oslo's government quarter, then traveled to Utøya Island where a youth camp was underway. Armed with multiple weapons and dressed in a fake police uniform, the bad guy systematically murdered sixty-nine people over ninety minutes. Most victims were teenagers. By day's end, seventy-seven people were dead and more than three hundred wounded.

Delta Norge, the Norwegian National Counterterrorism Unit, responded. As luck would have it, they couldn't get helicopters into the air because of thick fog. As a result, the team got there on a private boat they commandeered.

Once on the island the team quickly cleared everything, eventually locating the suspect. Holding him at gunpoint, their team leader saw that the suspect was wearing what appeared to be a bomb vest. The justification for lethal force was absolute. The team leader started to take up the slack in his trigger, to shoot the suspect.

But nanoseconds before the shot broke, he recognized that what he was seeing wasn't explosives. His finger came off the trigger. They took the suspect alive.

The professional restraint displayed in that moment, under those circumstances, was amazing. Bringing the suspect to justice without killing him became a source of lasting pride for the unit.

Years later, I asked this team leader what he was most proud of from that day. I really expected him to talk about the capture, about maintaining discipline when every fiber of his being wanted to pull that trigger, about bringing Norway's worst mass murderer to justice.

But he didn't mention any of that. What he said was this: "I am most proud of the guys in my team that actually did the medical assistance to all the people that needed it. They saved a bunch of lives, that's for sure, because that came back to my unit from the hospitals that got the injured people on their operation tables."

Given every opportunity to claim credit for one of the most consequential tactical operations in European history, this team leader immediately redirected to his teammates. Not his shot discipline. Not his leadership under fire. Not even their tactical abilities. His teammates and their medical work.

HOW TO START: OWNING THE LOSS

Think about your last significant win and your last significant loss. What language did you use to describe that to your team? Did they lose or did you? Did they win or did you take the credit?

How You Made Them Feel

On November 7, 2012, Jordan MacWilliams was a young officer on a Regional SWAT team. That morning, a domestic violence suspect had taken his ex-girlfriend hostage at gunpoint outside a casino in New Westminster, British Columbia. After a five-hour standoff, the suspect pointed a gun at the tactical team, and MacWilliams fired a single shot that killed him.

It was a completely justified shooting that occurred after hours of failed negotiations. He had fired only when the suspect pointed his gun toward the team and posed an imminent threat. By any reasonable standard, MacWilliams had done the right thing. He appeared to be clearly within the law and policy.

But then the nightmare began. The newly created Independent Investigations Office, a civilian police oversight board, charged him with second-degree murder. It was the first time a police officer had been charged for using lethal force in British Columbia since 1975 and MacWilliams was facing life in prison if convicted.

He languished for months awaiting court proceedings. When he received the disclosure package, he was aghast at the errors in the investigation. Shockingly, the investigators hadn't even interviewed the hostage. Eventually, the hostage went to the media when she saw that MacWilliams was being charged and the full picture began to emerge. The charges were eventually dropped.

Surprisingly, when I interviewed Jordan MacWilliams the thing that he described as most traumatic about this ordeal was not being charged with murder. It was the way his leadership treated him throughout. When Jordan needed his leadership most, they vanished. No one from his senior command staff reached out. No one publicly expressed support for him. The organization in which he had grown up, that had trained him and that had put him in that situation, now acted as if he was radioactive. They appeared to be protecting themselves and their careers, not MacWilliams. According to him, the highest-ranked person who sent him any note of support was a staff sergeant. Everyone above that rank went silent.

Years later, MacWilliams reflected on what had hurt him most: "I struggled for a little while with killing somebody. But the way my organization treated me kept me up for years and took my mental health into the garbage."

The poet Maya Angelou once famously said, "People will forget what you said, people will forget what you did, but people will never forget how you made them feel."

Think back to your childhood. Or more specifically to your memories from school. It is likely that you remember most clearly the traumatic events where someone humiliated you, embarrassed you, or treated you poorly in front of others. Memories have a strong root in emotions, and negative emotions are particularly strong.

This is especially important in leadership. Everyone has an asymmetrical relationship with their leadership at work. As a leader you have a profound ability to damage those you lead, and they have very little ability to damage you. You can take away their income, you can make their work life difficult, and you can undermine their sense of personal safety and security.

You may be the CEO of a business with 5,000 employees. You may not know 99 percent of their names. But every single one of them knows who you are, and as a result any interaction you have with them is profound. Treat them well, make them feel good, and they will remember that. Treat them poorly, embarrass them, or disregard their feelings, and they will never forget it.

But consider this: You can also be a source of support, of compassion, and of self-confidence. If you care about them and help them develop, they will give you 100 percent of what they have to give.

Seems like an easy choice, right? But it is surprising how often leaders get it wrong.

When Satya Nadella became CEO of Microsoft in 2014, he inherited a culture that had long been criticized for its internal competition, fear of failure, and siloed behaviors. Rather than supporting this notion of performance-at-all-costs, Nadella made empathy a core leadership principle. He reframed the company's identity from "know-it-alls" to "learn-it-alls," explicitly linking the mission to emotional intelligence.

Under Nadella, Microsoft moved away from a "zero-sum culture" toward one where psychological safety mattered. Employees were encouraged to share ideas, experiment, and fail without fear of punitive consequences.

During difficult organizational changes, including significant layoffs, Nadella repeatedly emphasized empathy and a growth mindset in internal communications, reminding employees that how they treated each other was as important as what they achieved.

What makes Nadella's example interesting is that empathy was not just a personal trait but also a governance mechanism. It shaped hiring, where collaboration and curiosity were valued alongside technical skill. It also shaped their promotions, where emotional intelligence really counted. This then shaped daily operations because leaders at all levels were encouraged to listen actively and to foster inclusion.

People will always remember how you make them feel. This is true whether you are a CEO, a middle manager, or a team member. It is also true as a parent and as a friend.

My primary objective is always to treat people well and to think about how my actions are impacting them, especially when their lives are in crisis. Leadership must be anchored in compassion, empathy, and genuine care for those you lead.

HOW TO START: BEING MAYA ANGELOU

Pick two people you have had a difficult personal situation under your leadership and ask them "Did you feel that we cared about you as a person?" Don't defend it, just listen. The gap between your intent and their experience is your growth area.

KEY PRINCIPLES

- Leaders are built, not born. The capacity to lead is forged through failure, training, and experience — not talent.
- Ego creates blind spots. Confidence is faith in your abilities. Ego is belief in your own superiority.
- Your job is to get the right answer, not have it. Stop being the answer and start finding people who are smarter than you.
- Own failures, share wins.
- People will forget what you said and did, but never forget how you made them feel.

What Comes Next

Servant leaders create the environment, but you cannot lead people into excellence. You must select for it. The next chapter explores how elite units find the right people in the first place: the rigorous, deliberate, sometimes painful process of kissing frogs enthusiastically until you find your prince.

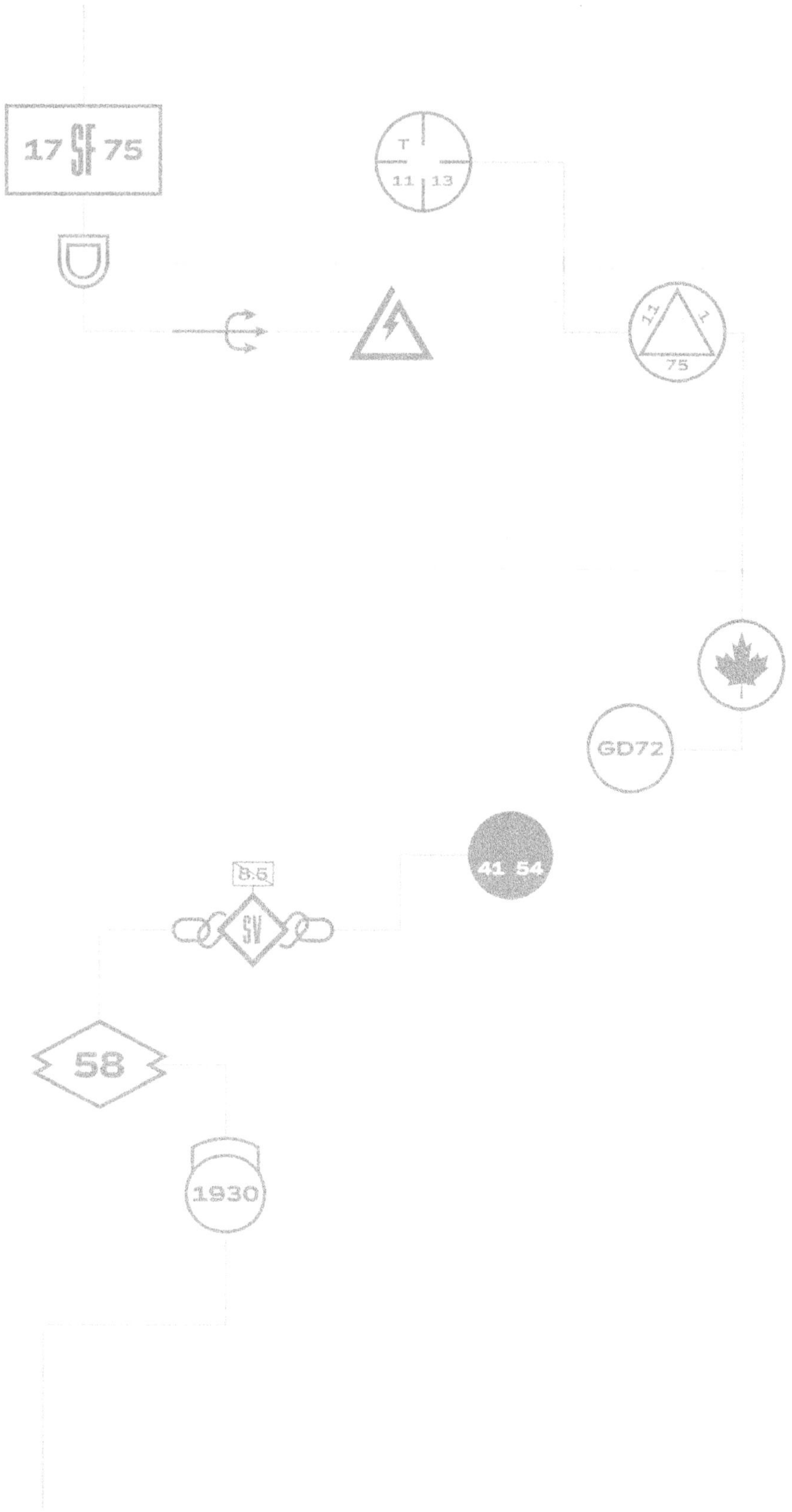
17 SF 75
T
11
13
11
1
75
GD72
41 54
SV
58
1930

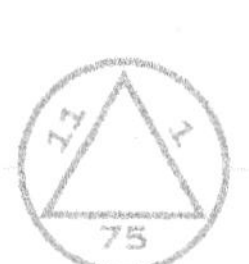

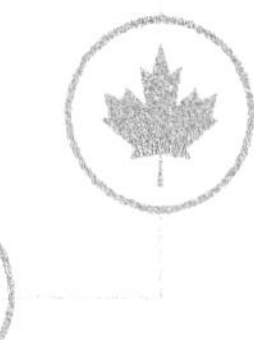

CHAPTER THREE

SELECT THE RIGHT PEOPLE

Kissing Frogs Enthusiastically

Somewhere in the mountains of West Virginia, a man is walking. He's been walking for sixteen hours. His rucksack weighs forty-five pounds, and he has no idea how far he has to go or whether he's meeting the standard. No one will tell him. At every checkpoint, an instructor simply acknowledges his presence, writes down his name, and then stares at him. In a calm voice the instructor suggests that he should quit. That it's hopeless, that there's no shame in quitting.

He won't quit. But of the 163 soldiers who started this course, only about ten or twelve will finish. Every single one of those 163 candidates was already an elite soldier: Rangers, Green Berets, men who have already proven themselves in the most demanding units in the Army. Yet more than 90 percent of them will fail. They will get hurt, their bodies will give out, or they will quit.

Welcome to Delta Force selection.

The American taxpayer invests between $5 and $10 million dollars to select and train a single Delta operator. Why would any organization invest that much? Certainly our tier 1 units require the absolute best of the best and there is no way to find that without a rigorous process. But that is not the only reason. The leadership of our tier 1 units understand something most business leaders will never learn: The cost of a bad hire will always exceed the cost of a longer search. Selection—aka hiring in the civilian world—is the single greatest input you have on your culture. As a result, it isn't an expense to minimize. It's an investment to make that will pay compounding returns for the years to come.

Yet most companies spend twenty minutes per candidate with a hiring manager and then check two references provided by the candidate. They hire for résumé and then fire for behavior. Then they wonder why their culture erodes.

The best organizations in the world would rather have an empty seat than fill it with the wrong person. That single principle separates elite teams from everyone else. The easiest place to protect culture is at the door—elite organizations are ruthless about who gets in because they know one wrong hire can destroy what took years to build.

In this chapter, I'll explore how elite organizations think about selection: how they define what they're looking for before they start evaluating, why culture is evaluated in addition to skill, how they build evaluation systems that actually work, why high individual performance can mask team destruction, what separates good evaluators from bad ones, and why selection never really ends for elite units.

Define the Prince

There is an old fairy tale about a princess who has to kiss a frog to turn it into a prince. In our organization, we use it as a metaphor for the search for new hires. In searching through lots of candidates to find the one we want, we like to say we are kissing frogs to find our prince. But please don't mistake that for a bad thing. Kissing frogs is the only way for us to find our prince!

To pick the right person, you first have to define what "right" looks like. John Dowd, a former SEAL and the founder of SOFware, LLC, has spent over fifteen years consulting with elite military and law enforcement units on their assessment and selection processes. Dowd and his team have created software and methodologies that many of the elite military units in the United States use to first define and then select the right people.

His first question to any client when they are planning selection is always the same: "Describe your aspirational culture." As he puts it, "Before thinking about candidates, I want them to think about themselves. For them to know whether a particular piece will fit into their team puzzle, we first need to know a great deal about the puzzle itself."

If this sounds like a deeply introspective journey for a hiring process, that's because it is. Understanding who you want is as much about you as it is about them.

Interestingly, the answer to this question is rarely clear. Units will say they want "leadership" or "mental toughness" or "team players." But these are not behaviors. They're abstract concepts that mean different things to different evaluators. As a result, selecting from these descriptions can lead to varying results.

Dowd's solution is what he calls the "gray beards" framework. Go find the high-reputation, experienced cultural agents in your organization: the people who've been there for years, who understand the mission at a cellular level. Then ask them: "For this role, what concrete observable behaviors did you witness that made a difference?"

Behaviors. Not "leadership" but "took initiative when the group lacked direction." Not "mental toughness" but "remained composed when facing hostile questions." Not "team player" but "voluntarily helped teammates complete their tasks without being asked." Behaviors can be observed, measured, and compared across candidates. Abstract concepts cannot.

Steve Jobs seemingly understood this instinctively. When asked about what his role was at Apple, he said, "My number one job here at Apple is to make sure that the top 100 people are A-plus players. And everything else will take care of itself." Jobs didn't delegate hiring decisions for critical roles to others. He personally interviewed candidates, sometimes spending hours with a single person to ensure they were the right fit. He wasn't looking for credentials. He was looking for specific behaviors that indicated someone belonged.

Your organization has gray beards. Find them and ask what behaviors they think matter. Then use those behaviors to define what your prince is like before you start kissing frogs.

Try to establish a clear list of the kinds of behaviors and skills you want for a position before you start assessing people. Not a list of the job duties but a list of what the ideal candidate looks like. After all, you cannot find the right person if you do not know what right looks like. Define your prince!

> **HOW TO START: BUILDING YOUR PRINCE**
>
> Make a list of your key values and translate them into observable behaviors. "Integrity" may be "admits mistakes immediately" and "raises concerns early." Then assess whether you are seeing those behaviors. If you can't observe it, you can't select for it.

Buy vs. Build

Once you have defined your prince, there's a fundamental question that every selection process needs to answer: What do we need to "buy" in a candidate and what are we able to "build" in them?

Buy means the candidates must already possess this quality when they walk through the door. This trait cannot be built with the time and resources available. Build means that we can develop it through training and experience. The difference here really matters because it determines what your minimum threshold for selection is for different behaviors and characteristics.

For example, if we are hiring a racing jockey to ride our racehorse, they will have to be very small and very light. We cannot possibly develop those things. So we cannot hire a six foot tall 300-pound man and expect him to become the jockey. The same would be true for a surgeon who must have the requisite training and licensing before we hire her. There are certain things that the candidates simply must have when they walk in the door because building them would either be impossible or too expensive or time-consuming.

Dowd's team categorizes selection criteria into three steps:

1. What's the minimum required proficiency?
2. Can this behavior be developed?
3. Given the finite time and resources we have available, how much can we build, and therefore what's the minimum level we need at selection?

Physical fitness provides an easy example. If you need someone who can run a 6 minute mile, and you will have eight weeks to train the person up to that level after hiring them. Running is something that can be developed, so you could hire someone who runs a mile in six minute and thirty seconds and train them to the six minute standard.

We can buy at 6:30 and build to 6:00. But in the time we have available we can't buy at 10:00 and build to 6:00.

This is where most organizations go wrong because they think about this type of framework for technical skills but ignore it for character and team impact. Technical skills generally live in the build column. Character mostly lives in the buy column.

Although the right culture can often enhance the integrity and character of team members, there is no training program that instills integrity. So, if you don't buy it when you hire people, they simply will not have it.

Dowd puts it more bluntly: "You can be tough and toxic." A candidate can pass every physical test, can demonstrate all the required technical competence, and still be absolutely wrong for your team.

Competence isn't the same as suitability. Individual performance isn't the same as team contribution. You are looking for the right person not the best person.

One of my friends who commands a top tier unit describes it this way: "We had a guy show up who could shoot like John Wick and who looked like Jean-Claude Van Damme. But he was the most caustic personality we have ever run across, and we cut him in selection. The unit he went to thought they were getting a steal. Within weeks, they were trying to get rid of him. They bought best; we were looking for right."

This became Netflix's foundational insight, and their policy became explicit: "On our dream team, there are no brilliant jerks, as they are detrimental to great teamwork."

HOW TO START: BUY V. BUILD

Take your most common role and list every quality you want. Sort each into Buy (must walk in the door with it) or Build (you can develop it). Your Buy column is your non-negotiable selection criteria.

Own the Yardstick

Once you know what you're looking for, you need a way to measure it. This is where most selection processes fall apart because they measure what's easy rather than what matters.

All tests for selection or hiring fall into one of two types, quantitative or qualitative. There are significant differences between how they are each measured and the results they will provide.

Quantitative assessments are used for traits that can be counted, timed, or measured without judgment: pushups, run times, test scores, credentials, licenses. They're objective and repeatable, and different evaluators will measure them in the same way. They are therefore safe for any evaluator to administer.

Qualitative assessments, on the other hand, require evaluator judgment: leadership, teamwork, communication, composure under pressure. They're subjective, variable, and require a common definition or they will yield varying and inconsistent results. These can be unreliable and therefore dangerous in the hands of the wrong evaluator.

The problem is that the most important selection criteria (team impact, character, cultural fit) are usually qualitative and therefore harder to measure. The less important (physical performance, technical knowledge, etc) are usually quantitative and therefore easier to measure. As a result, organizations naturally drift toward measuring what's easy to measure, which means overweighting individual performance on technical skills and underweighting team impact and character. It also leads to overweighting credentials, degrees, and accomplishments and underweighting how the person will fit into the team culture.

To put this into context, skills and capabilities may predict how well someone can do the job, but they do not accurately predict how well they will work with the team, and the latter is far more important.

Owning the yardstick means taking control of your evaluation standards rather than defaulting to convenient metrics. It means investing in the harder work of qualitative assessment for character, integrity, and team impact, because that's where the real signal lives.

Amazon utilizes a cultural veto system that they call the Bar Raiser program. For over two decades, Amazon has used specially trained employee volunteers who serve as objective third-party assessors during hiring. These Bar Raisers undergo six to twelve months of intensive preparation. They sit on interview panels for teams other than their own, have no stake in whether the position gets filled, and focus solely on whether the candidate meets Amazon's standards.

The Bar Raiser's singular question: Will this person raise the bar? Is he or she better than at least 50 percent of current Amazonians in similar roles? If the answer is no, the hire doesn't happen.

Here's the critical detail: The Bar Raiser has veto power. If they determine a candidate doesn't meet Amazon's standards, the hire doesn't happen regardless of how urgently the team needs to fill the role. The system works because it separates the need to fill a position from the authority to approve a hire. Hiring managers feel pressure to get someone in the seat. The Bar Raiser has no such pressure. Their only job is to protect the standard.

We adopted a system for this starting many years ago. In our hiring process we pay a little attention to your résumé, degrees, and such measures. But we pay a great deal of attention to who you are and how you will fit.

To accomplish this we utilize multiple interviews. Although you may have one technical interview, which will usually be with HR or your supervisor, you will likely have several culture interviews.

In these culture interviews you will see a variety of different people from a variety of different departments and demographics. In some of these contexts you may not even realize what is happening is part of the formal interview process. For example, you may not realize that the receptionist who greets you is actually one of your evaluators.

The rule for these evaluators is that none of them have the ability to hire you. But all of them can eliminate you if they think you are a threat to our culture.

Simply put, this has been the most effective hiring tool that we have ever used. It enables us to focus on who you are as a person. It also gives us the perspectives of a variety of different people and a look at how you treat different team members. It never ceases to amaze me how many people never make it past the receptionist because they treat their potential boss well but are dismissive or rude to those they see as being below them.

For shorter selection processes, multiple interviews spread over time with a variety of people seem to be the most effective approach. You need to look at the person through a variety of lenses over time if possible. Anyone can be nice for a few minutes; the question is what happens when the mask comes off.

Own your yardstick by deciding what your evaluation methods will be and then building independence into your evaluation process. Use multiple assessors. Include people from outside the hiring team. Give someone the explicit job of protecting standards, with the authority to say no. Your culture is most dependent on the subjective aspects, so pay attention to them. If not, you may hire a high-performing asshole.

HOW TO START:
SELECTING FOR WHAT WORKS

Write down every key trait used in your last three hires. Circle the ones that actually predicted success or failure in that role. Did the way you measured them actually select for things that matter?

Avoid the High-Performing Asshole

For many years I have been fascinated by the selection processes of elite units. Although there are a lot of common characteristics among teams, it was difficult to pin down exactly what they were really looking for.

So one night over dinner with a friend who served in one of these elite units, I decided to dive deep into this topic.

"What exactly are you looking for when hiring?" I asked.

He took several swings at an answer. They're smart, team players, good people.

But each time, his explanations were met with me saying, "Yeah, I get that, but I want to know exactly what you're looking for."

He grew frustrated with my insistence and finally uttered a phrase that struck me like lightning: "We're just trying to avoid picking high-performing assholes."

That was it. The ideal selection for any high-performing team isn't just about hiring high performers. It's about avoiding the hiring of high performers who can't get along with others and will destroy the team culture.

HPAs are usually extremely high performers with strong résumés and successful personas. The high performance isn't the problem. The essential element is the A. HPAs are selfish and narcissistic. They win by making others lose. Simply put, HPAs are toxic for their coworkers and, worse yet, toxic for their organizations.

Early in my career, I had the opportunity to hire a star sales guy. He was a top sales performer at a competitor, had a résumé that read like a highlight reel, and brought with him the tantalizing prospect of not only growing my business but also hurting a rival.

The problem: I didn't like him.

He was condescending and arrogant. During our interviews, he made it clear that he believed he was doing me a favor by considering my company. My gut told me he would have a negative impact on our culture. But his qualifications were undeniable, and the siren song of stealing market share was too strong to resist.

I hired him. It was one of the worst decisions I've ever made.

Within months, everyone in the organization hated him. He was a morale cancer. Yes, he could sell. But the damage he did to our team culture far outweighed any revenue he brought in. People avoided meetings where he'd be present. Collaboration died. Junior employees who used to speak up went silent.

The end came less than a year after he started. I found him standing over a female coworker at her desk, invading her personal space, jamming his finger in her face while berating her. She was clearly frightened. He was completely out of control. I had traded company culture for qualifications, and it was a terrible deal.

John Dowd's research provides a means of avoiding the HPA. His team categorizes selection criteria into three buckets:

- **Individual Performance** - what people achieve on their own
- **Team Impact** - how they affect the people around them
- **Community Devotion** - their commitment to organizational values over personal gain

Individual performance is the easiest to measure and the most frequently overmeasured. Team impact is the hardest to measure and therefore the most frequently ignored. Yet team impact is the most important to your culture. Community devotion can really only be measured over time, so it is challenging for selection.

Google's Project Oxygen research confirmed this at scale. Analyzing data from hundreds of teams, they discovered that of the eight behaviors that mattered most for manager effectiveness, only one related to technical expertise. The other seven were all about how the person affected others. Technical brilliance ranked lowest. Team impact ranked highest.

How do you spot an HPA before you hire one? Dowd recommends peer surveys during extended selection processes. Peers see what evaluators miss: how the candidate treats people when no authority figure is watching, whether they help others without being asked, whether they add energy to the group or drain it. The peer survey question that matters most: Would you want to work with this person again?

Over the years I have seen a variety of approaches to ferreting out team impact:

- Giving small groups of candidates a team task to perform together and watching how they relate to each other.
- Giving candidates a task that they cannot possibly succeed at to see how they react to failure.
- Placing someone in the waiting room from the team to chat up the potential candidates.
- Making them wait for an extended period of time to see how they react.

There are myriad ways to look for the essence of who someone is. The main point is understanding that if you are not specifically selecting for their impact on your team, you are setting yourself up to hire an HPA.

HOW TO START: IDENTIFYING YOUR HPAS

Write down the people who deliver results but leave damaged relationships behind them. For each one, list who has left because of them and how much management time is spent on their fallout. The performance they deliver almost never exceeds the damage.

Santa, Gatekeeper, or Sensei

Your selection process is ultimately only as good as your evaluators. And not all evaluators are created equal. Who you choose to decide what's right for you can have as much impact on the process as what they ask or have the candidates do.

John Dowd and his team have observed thousands of selection cadre members across elite units and identified three distinct archetypes: gatekeepers, Santas, and senseis.

The **gatekeeper** is the bitter veteran with impossibly high standards. No one is ever good enough for them. The gatekeeper under-selects because admitting a new person means admitting that someone else could possibly meet their standards. They take pride in how many candidates they've rejected, treating selection as a demonstration of their own toughness rather than as a search for the right people. This yields false negatives—people not selected who should be.

The Santa is the opposite problem: too lenient, too quick to see potential, too reluctant to deliver negative news. Santas overselect because saying no feels mean. They focus on what candidates could become rather than what they are, rationalizing weaknesses as growth opportunities. This yields false positives—people who are selected and should not be.

The **sensei** is the gold standard: rigorous but developmental, demanding but fair. The sensei is motivated to find the right candidates, not to reject everyone or accept everyone. They can deliver hard truths with respect. They understand that high standards and human decency aren't in conflict.

The application for hiring is straightforward: always restrict gatekeepers and Santas to objective, quantitative measurements where their biases can't contaminate the assessment. Reserve qualitative assessments (leadership, teamwork, cultural fit) for your senseis.

When it comes to the final call on cultural fit, only senseis should have a vote. Gatekeepers and Santas can assess what's measurable. Senseis assess what matters.

Amazon's Bar Raiser program is essentially a sensei factory. Those months of training are about developing the judgment, calibration, and mindset that senseis possess naturally. Amazon recognized that evaluator quality isn't random. It can be cultivated.

Dowd frames this as the cadre's being a compounding investment. Candidates who pass through selection carry the imprint of their evaluators for their entire career. If your cadre is made up of senseis, that quality compounds across every successful candidate. If your cadre is contaminated with gatekeepers or Santas, that dysfunction compounds too.

HOW TO START: CHOOSING THE RIGHT EVALUATORS

For everyone directly involved in your hiring process, ask: Do they reject almost everyone (Gatekeeper), approve almost everyone (Santa), or assess objectively against clear criteria (Sensei)? Make sure your final decisions are made by Senseis.

Earn This Every Day

Elite teams are unique in many ways, but perhaps none are as obvious as their professionalism. The members of elite organizations take their jobs, and their roles in their units, very seriously. There is nothing taken for granted. Professionalism permeates everything they do. Everything is studied, plans are agonized over, written documents are produced at a high level, and gear is well cared for. In their world, you're always trying out for your job. Failing a physical training exam can end your time with the unit. Failing a firearms qualification can end your time with the unit. A pattern of poor judgment, even if no single incident is disqualifying, can end your time with the unit. Simply put, all details are suffered over and every day you are earning the privilege of being in the unit.

This is not unique to tactical units either. This is common among all elite organizations. Throughout my career I have had the opportunity to get inside looks at everything from the Ferrari Formula 1 team to Broadway shows, and from professional sports teams to high-tech companies. The one constant I have found among the best, no matter the arena, is professionalism. Everyone is trying to always do the best job possible. Nothing is left to chance.

Chief Phil Hansen summed this up for me in our interview. Phil spent nearly twenty years as a team leader and team commander in the Los Angeles County Sheriff's Department Special Enforcement Bureau, one of the premier tactical units in American law enforcement. He describes this phenomenon in a single simple phrase: "You've got to earn this team, and you've got to earn it every day."

Every day. Not once, when you pass selection. Not periodically, when evaluation cycles come around. Every single day, you prove you belong. Your past performance earns you nothing except the opportunity to perform again tomorrow.

This might sound exhausting. But it's very liberating. When membership is earned daily, no one rests on reputation. No one coasts on previous accomplishments. The senior person with twenty years of experience and the newcomer with twenty months operate under the same standard: What did you bring today?

Netflix built their entire talent philosophy around this concept. In their famous culture deck, they're explicit: "Adequate performance gets a generous severance package." That sounds harsh until you understand the logic. If past performance entitled employees to continued employment regardless of current contribution, you'd create an organization where the best people subsidize the average ones. The best people eventually leave, tired of carrying weight that isn't pulling itself. What remains is a culture of entitlement masquerading as loyalty.

The earning never stops because the mission never stops. Markets change. Threats evolve. What made you valuable yesterday might be irrelevant tomorrow. The only response is continuous demonstration of value, continuous commitment to growth, continuous proof that you deserve to be here.

John Dowd captures this with a phrase he learned from his friend Hans Hansen: "Your whole career is a selection event."

You are always in a process of being evaluated for future responsibilities. You are always being measured against the standards for the unit. And you are always aware that failing to meet standards will result in your leaving. As a result, you had better be professional and focused on what matters.

This is not meant to imply that every day you are at risk for being removed from your job. That would just create anxiety and make people feel insecure. No, it's about maintaining the standards that made the unit elite in the first place. The same rigor that filtered candidates during initial selection continues to apply to them throughout their tenure. The bar doesn't drop just because you're inside the tent.

Netflix operationalized this principle with what they call the Keeper Test. Managers are expected to regularly ask themselves: "If this person told me they were leaving for a similar job at another company, would I fight hard to keep them?" If the answer is no, Netflix's position is clear: Give them a generous severance and let them go.

The Keeper Test sounds harsh, and perhaps it is. But it reflects a truth that most organizations avoid confronting: adequate isn't good enough. Someone can be meeting expectations, not causing problems, doing their job reasonably well, and still be wrong for the team. That person is taking a spot that could be filled by someone better.

Most organizations treat hiring as the selection moment and then stop selecting. Performance reviews happen annually, if at all. Feedback is vague and backward-looking. The standard that candidates had to meet to get hired becomes a ceiling rather than a floor.

Earn this every day means continuous evaluation against your standards. It means giving honest feedback regularly, not annually. It means having the courage to acknowledge when someone isn't working out, even if the employee is not technically failing. The organizations that take selection seriously never stop selecting. The bar that lets you in is the same bar you clear every day.

HOW TO START: ARE YOU EARNING IT EVERY DAY?

List five behaviors that distinguish a professional from someone just showing up in your team. Grade yourself against them honestly. Are you earning your position every day or are you coasting? Your team will never exceed the standard you personally demonstrate.

KEY PRINCIPLES

- Define the prince before you start kissing frogs. Know exactly who you are looking for before you start looking.
- Buy vs. Build: Know when to hire for culture fit and develop skills versus hire for skills and hope for culture fit.
- Own the yardstick. Control your selection standards and process, or someone else will lower them for yours.
- Avoid the high-performing asshole. Toxic talent destroys more than it creates. The performance is never worth the price.
- Be a sensei, not a Santa or a gatekeeper. Balance high standards with genuine investment in people's development.
- Selection never stops. How people perform every day is still the selection process. Earn this every day.

What Comes Next

Selection gets the right people in the door. But those people must be strong, not compliant. Passion is the raw material of excellence, and it's easier to temper passion than to inspire it. The next challenge is building a team of people who will challenge you, push back, and tell you what you're missing.

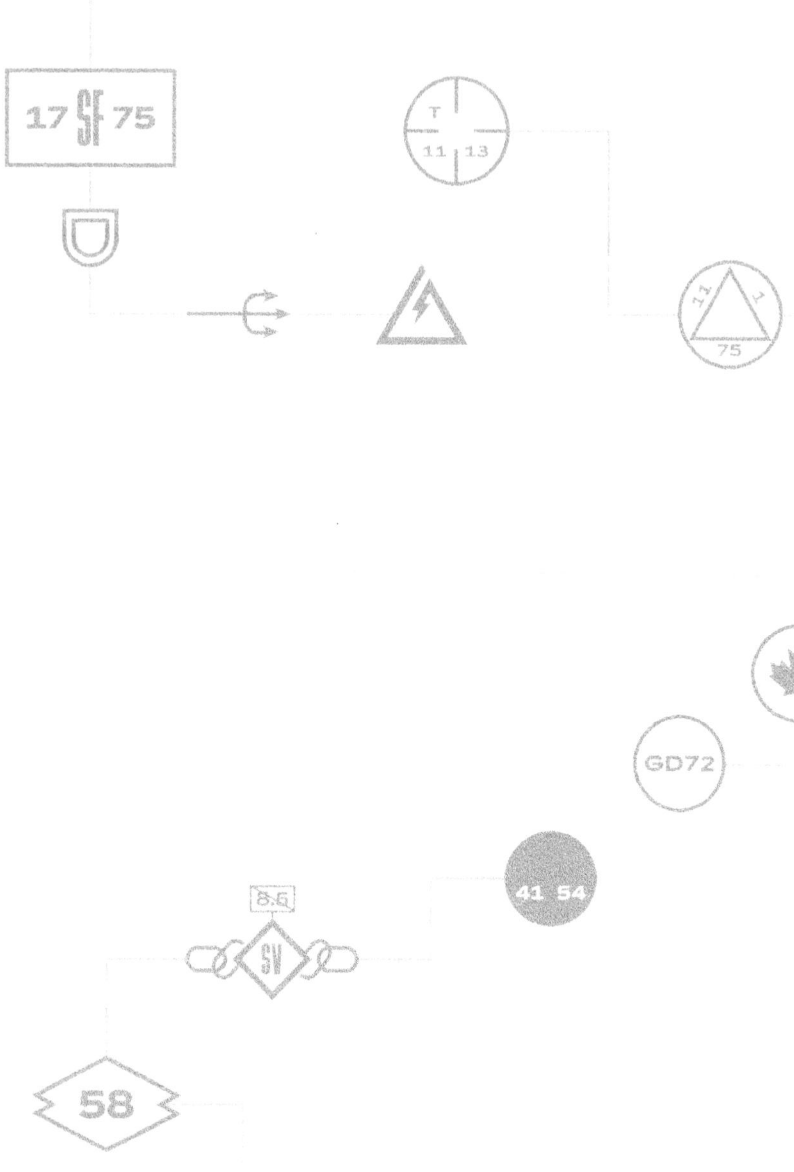

CHAPTER FOUR

EMBRACE STRONG PEOPLE

Knives Not Spoons

On August 6, 1997, Korean Air flight 801 approached Guam's airport in poor weather. The captain was tired and making errors. The first officer could see they were in trouble. He knew they were descending too fast and that the captain's approach was wrong. He knew disaster was approaching: Bijia Peak.

But Korean culture at that time had extremely high levels of power distance, meaning subordinates did not question superiors. The first officer made some mild suggestions and hinted at problems, but he never directly challenged the captain's decisions. The plane crashed into the hillside three miles short of the runway. Two hundred twenty-nine people died because a subordinate could not speak plainly to his superior about an obvious problem. Research into this and similar crashes has identified a clear pattern: The cultures that produced the deadliest cockpits were cultures where subordinates could not challenge authority, where hierarchy mattered more than the truth did.

The lesson for organizational leaders is clear: a hierarchy that prevents truth from reaching decision-makers is a hierarchy that kills the organization. Perhaps not literally in most business contexts unless you are flying a 747, but it kills initiatives, kills innovation, kills the organization's ability to adapt to changing circumstances. Your organization has people who can see when you are making mistakes. The question is whether they feel safe telling you.

One of the most valuable leadership lessons I learned came from watching one of my junior staff members publicly challenge an expensive consultant I had hired and then directly attack my thinking in front of my entire team. The experience taught me something that decades of working with elite tactical units had been trying to show me: The people who make you uncomfortable are often the people you need most.

Several years ago, I decided to certify our company to the ISO9001 international quality standard. It was a daunting task for a business our size, and I hired an experienced consultant to guide us through the process. He was a confident man in his sixties with the swagger of someone who had been there and done that, and he showed little interest in the opinions of others.

During one of our early meetings, a young woman named Milena, who was three levels below me in the organization, began questioning his approach. Her inquiries, initially rooted in curiosity, gradually became more aggressive and confrontational during the meeting. At the break, she approached me and said she did not like his answers and planned to do some research of her own that night.

The next day, she arrived ready for battle. She systematically challenged his opinions until, by lunch, the atmosphere had grown so tense that I asked her to stop. In response, she told me I should fire the consultant, build our own program, and let her create and manage it herself. This was more than bold. It was a direct challenge to my plan, my choice of consultant, and the organizational hierarchy I had established.

My initial reaction was embarrassment and anger that my leadership was being challenged so directly. Yet as I considered the situation more carefully, I realized this was precisely the kind of culture we needed to create.

More importantly, she was right. I had picked the wrong consultant. At the end of the day, we fired the consultant, developed our own program, and put her in charge. This proved to be the right decision. She crushed the project and created a far better program than we had expected. She also earned a two-step promotion to become a company director, reporting directly to me, which she still does today.

It would have been easy to shut her down that day to protect my ego and my pride. If I had done that, I would have not only made a mistake on that project, but I would also have silenced one of the strongest voices in my organization. I also would have damaged the organization as a whole.

Successful organizations are built from groups of passionate people who push each other hard, challenge their leadership to make them better, and communicate directly and effectively with one another. The best leaders encourage passion and foster an environment open to strong disagreement, while demanding mutual respect among the participants.

Feed the Fire

Early in my career I had the privilege of attending the internal debrief of a unit on the East Coast. They were debriefing an incident that had gone quite poorly, and the discussion was contentious. To say the least, there was a strong difference of opinion on what had gone wrong, and the two sides were passionately arguing about it. The room was so tense it felt like a fistfight might break out at any time.

This was not my first time witnessing one of these disagreements, but it was certainly the most uncomfortable. The discussion went on for quite some time, but eventually the argument was settled with an agreement on what changes they would make. Followed by a big bear hug. The team then went to lunch and acted as though nothing had happened.

At lunch the unit commander asked me what I thought of the debrief. I told him I really thought it was going to end in a fight. He laughed and said, "No, pal, they're just Italian. Besides they all just really care a lot."

Then he uttered a magic phrase: "It is always easier to temper passion than it is to inspire it!"

I instantly got a glimpse of the key ingredient for great teams: passionate people.

Passionate people care deeply about what they do. They work hard and obsess over little details. They learn deeply about the things they care about and are often the source of innovation. They are the star performers of the organization and the centers of creation and of excellence.

However, passionate people usually have sharp edges. They are constantly looking for a better way and are frequently frustrated by others. They speak truth to power more often than not, and they don't suffer fools kindly. This can make them a real handful for leaders.

Sadly, many leaders interpret passionate people as "difficult personalities" and become frustrated. They find such individuals hard to control, argumentative, and sometimes disrespectful. In many business environments, this leads to "truth tellers" being marginalized, disciplined, or even fired.

Passion is quashed in favor of obedience. Conformity is encouraged through words and actions, with an eye toward producing a homogeneous team where everyone plays nice and does what they are told.

This approach is like throwing away all the sharp knives in your kitchen to avoid injuring yourself. Sure, you will certainly be safer, but you will also end up with a drawer full of spoons. Spoons are great, they work together well, they nest nicely in the drawer, and no one has ever cut themselves with a spoon.

If all you want the organization to do is metaphorically "eat soup"—aka underperform—then spoons are fine. But if you want a "meat-eating team" that achieves at a high level, then you have to have knives. This means feeding the fire of passionate people and encouraging them to be themselves.

As Jeff Bezos likes to note about Amazon, their culture is "friendly and intense, but if push comes to shove, we'll settle for intense."

One additional point deserves emphasis: Passionate does not mean loud. Some of the most passionate people I have encountered are quiet and reserved. They sit in the back of the room and rarely dominate meetings. But that doesn't mean they are not fiery on the inside. Don't confuse aggression with passion; they are different. The best accounting, IT, or research staff are often reserved, but they are also passionate.

Leaders should never mistake volume for strength or silence for weakness.

HOW TO START: BUILDING AN ARGUMENT

In your next team meeting, deliberately propose an idea you know has weaknesses or won't work. See if anyone pushes back. If the room goes silent or immediately agrees, your people are likely placating you, not collaborating with you.

Don't Be the Emperor – Question Authority

You know the story. The emperor parades through the streets in his magnificent new clothes. Everyone can see he is naked, but nobody says anything. The weavers have convinced everyone that only fools cannot see the fabric, so the courtiers praise the garments, the citizens applaud, and the emperor walks on, exposed and oblivious, until a child finally states the obvious.

Most organizations have emperors, and most of those emperors do not know they are naked. The question every leader must ask is whether they have created conditions where someone would tell them if they knew he was naked.

Remember Milena from the opening of this chapter. My first instinct was to shut her down, to protect my ego, to maintain hierarchy, to support the expensive consultant I had hired. If I had followed that instinct, I would have been the emperor: exposed and oblivious. She was like the child willing to state the obvious.

The most valuable person in your organization is often the one willing to tell you that you are wrong. Not the sycophants who tell you what you want to hear. Not the politicians who protect their positions by protecting yours. No, the truth teller, the one who risks your displeasure because they care more about the mission than about your comfort.

Bob Koonce commanded *USS Key West* (SSN-722), a Los Angeles–class nuclear attack submarine, for the United States Navy. He served on five different nuclear fast attack boats over a twenty-year career and is one of the most experienced submarine officers in the fleet. When I interviewed him he described something that initially seemed paradoxical.

"When we first built nuclear submarines back in the early 1950s," Koonce explained, "Admiral Hyman

Rickover realized that he couldn't have the standard old school military concept: top down, do as you're told, don't question authority, just follow procedures without thinking." Instead, Rickover created a culture built on what the submarine community calls "questioning attitude" and "watch team backup."

Here's how Koonce describes it: "We tell sailors to follow procedures, be very formal, but then we say: And now, question everything. Question your commanding officer because he might make a mistake. Question your executive officer. She might make a mistake. Question the procedure. It could be wrong. Question the equipment. It could be operating incorrectly. You're constantly told to question everything around you because something's trying to kill you."

On a nuclear submarine, that's literally true. You're 800 feet underwater. The pressure is crushing. You're operating a nuclear reactor, managing torpedoes and missiles. Any of a hundred things can fail catastrophically. The only way to survive is to have every member of the crew actively looking for problems, regardless of rank or role.

But Koonce is careful to distinguish this from anarchy: "That questioning attitude is critical, but we can't have anarchy also, so all those things have to work kind of in harmony." The goal isn't rebellion. It's a culture where following direction and questioning authority coexist, where people are simultaneously disciplined enough to execute orders and confident enough to speak up when something seems wrong.

Rickover understood that in complex, high-stakes environments, the person closest to the problem is usually the one who sees it first. This also frequently happens to be the lowest ranking person in the group whose opinion is easy to ignore. But a hierarchy that silences those voices doesn't create order. It creates a catastrophe waiting to happen.

Ed Catmull, the co-founder of Pixar built their creative culture around the same principle. In *Creativity, Inc.*, he describes how Pixar's "Brain Trust" meetings work: Directors present in-progress films to peers who tear the work apart with brutal honesty. No punches pulled. No hierarchy protection. The only rule is that criticism must be constructive and directed at the work, not the person. The results speak for themselves. Pixar had hit after hit for decades, in an industry where most studios struggled to repeat success even once.

This really matters for what comes later in this book where I explore collaborative decision-making in detail. But it is important to know that you will never get genuine collaborative input if team members don't already have a cultural foundation of healthy irreverence and a willingness to question authority. The best teammates question authority because they care more about getting the right answer than they do about looking good or avoiding conflict. They speak up because staying silent would let their team fail, which is culturally unacceptable.

As a leader, this is best case scenario for getting the right answer. Don't be the emperor! Surround yourself with people who will speak truth to power.

HOW TO START:
QUESTIONING AUTHORITY

In your last five team meetings, how many times did someone openly disagree with a proposed direction? If the answer is zero, your team is either perfect or afraid.

Candor Without Cruelty

Part of the reason I enjoy the tactical community is their ability to speak candidly and directly. Team members are expected to speak their minds to one another in an unvarnished and direct way. This doesn't mean being cruel or rude, it means not sugarcoating the truth because doing so dilutes the message. These conversations are not always comfortable. Candid conversations rarely are. But they are essential and underlie a healthy culture and effective communication.

Sadly, as a society, we have moved away from the time when someone who was underperforming would have a supervisor take them aside and say directly, "You are struggling, and you need to improve." We avoid such conversations now because people get their feelings hurt, because they do not feel safe when confronted, and because direct feedback makes them uncomfortable. So, in most organizations, instead of having the difficult conversation early, they wait until an employee or team member fails badly and then fire them.

This is a terrible approach to leadership. If the goal is to harness the full potential of every person in your organization, you need to be able to have difficult conversations early. You also need to say clearly that something is not working before it becomes unfixable.

Elite units tend to excel at this practice. They are skilled at having conversations that begin with, "Your performance is slipping. Are you okay? Is everything all right?" The conversation might start with humor, but as someone approaches the edge of the standard, the feedback becomes more direct: "We want you to be here, but your performance this month was below standard. You need to address this."

Ed Catmull built one of the most successful creative cultures in history around this principle. As he puts it: "A hallmark of a healthy creative culture is that its people feel free to share ideas, opinions, and criticisms. Lack of candor, if unchecked, ultimately leads to dysfunctional environments."

Pixar's Brain Trust meetings are legendary for their frank, candid feedback on works in progress. The system works because feedback is given without authority. The creative team retains full ownership. Problems can be pointed out without politics or posturing. This is the same dynamic that makes elite tactical teams effective: the ability to say what needs to be said without destroying relationships.

Direct candid feedback appears harsh. But the organization's knives are only sharpened by friction. The blade and the stone have what appear to be a harsh relationship, but the blade is only made sharper by the friction of the stone.

The key factor is that the candor and feedback must be rooted in care and a genuine desire to improve the person. Communication in elite units is direct and at times even brutally honest, but it is never cruel and never bullying. These are not the same and the difference really matters.

Gregg Popovich, the legendary NBA coach, was notorious for his brutal honesty with players. As one of his assistants explained: "He'll tell you the truth, with no BS, and then he'll love you to death." The honesty works because it comes wrapped in genuine care.

Somewhat paradoxically, direct communication often creates more psychological safety rather than less. The alternative of wondering what the boss really thinks, waiting for consequences that never come, or never knowing if performance is acceptable is what destroys people over time.

Harvard professor Amy Edmondson distinguishes between being nice and being kind. Nice avoids discomfort. Kind serves the other person's genuine interest, even when that is uncomfortable. The nice boss lets performance slide to avoid awkwardness. The kind boss has the difficult conversation because they genuinely care about the person's development and future.

HOW TO START: THE AWKWARD CONVERSATION

Write down every performance issue or unresolved conflict you've been putting off. Are they getting better on their own or are you avoiding the awkward chat? Schedule the most urgent one this week.

Passionate People Not HPAs

As we discussed in the last chapter, one significant threat to an organization of high performers is hiring that high-performing asshole. It is essential that we now differentiate between strong people and HPAs.

There is a significant difference between strong individuals who challenge leadership to make the organization better and toxic personalities who damage everything they touch. Between someone who wants the team to win and someone who wants to make others lose. Between a passionate person and an HPA.

In *The Culture Code*, Daniel Coyle describes research by Will Felps on what he called the bad apple effect. Felps placed an actor trained to play negative archetypes into working groups. In almost every case, that single negative person reduced group performance by 30 to 40 percent, regardless of which negative role he played. The toxicity was contagious.

Here is how I think about the distinction. Passionate people are knives—sharp and capable of cutting—but they accomplish the work that needs to be done in support of the team. High-performing assholes are not knives. They are broken glass. They cut indiscriminately, including cutting the team and the organization.

You can develop high performance through training. You cannot train away toxicity. The strong personality who challenges your ideas because they want the organization to succeed deserves embrace and cultivation. This is the employee who will speak up if they perceive the organization is flying into a hillside. The toxic personality who tears others down because it makes them feel powerful requires removal.

HOW TO START:
PASSIONATE PEOPLE NOT HPAS

Think of the strongest personality on your team — the one who pushes back, challenges ideas, and makes meetings uncomfortable. Now ask honestly: are they making the organization better or are they making others smaller? If it's the former, are you embracing them or managing them down? If it's the latter, what are you waiting for?

KEY PRINCIPLES

- It is always easier to temper passion than it is to inspire it. Find the people who are on fire and feed the flame.
- Strong personalities are assets, not problems—if you selected right.
- Candor without cruelty: Direct feedback is kindness; avoiding hard conversations is cowardice.
- Knives and broken glass both cut. Passionate people challenge the mission to make it better. HPAs cut indiscriminately. Only one belongs on your team.
- Don't be the emperor with no clothes—create conditions where people tell you the truth.

What Comes Next

Passionate people generally like having something to measure themselves against. Without clear standards, even the most driven performers will drift. They will lose their edge because there is nothing to sharpen themselves against. Without benchmarks to strive for, or a line that separates acceptable from excellent, even high performers will lose their way. The best team members don't just tolerate high standards, they crave them.

The next chapter examines how elite teams establish and maintain those standards, and why the standards you tolerate always matter more than the standards you articulate.

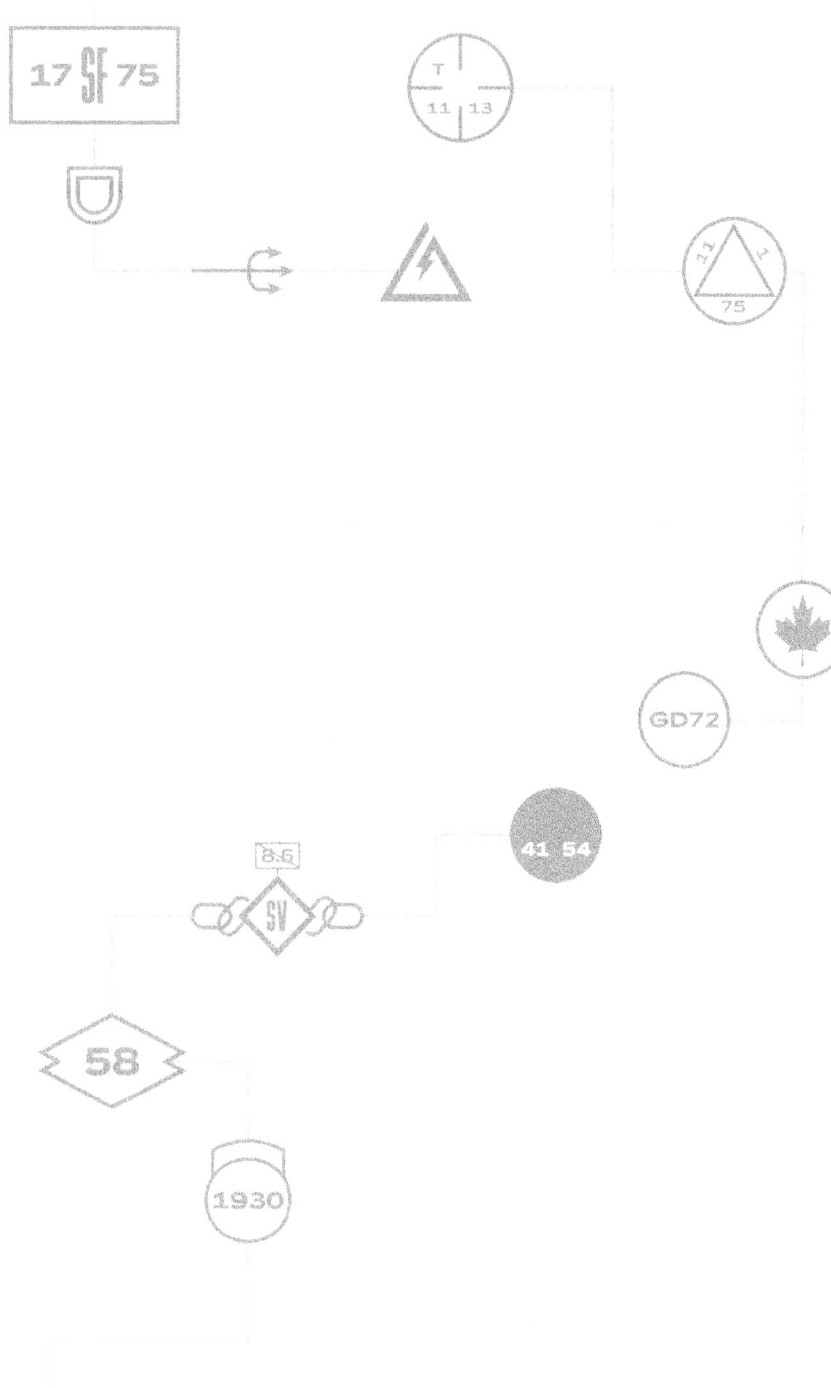

CHAPTER FIVE

ENFORCE HIGH STANDARDS

What You Tolerate is Your Standard

At 2:00 a.m. on September 5, 2005, a 52,000-ton Turkish freighter hit the American Navy submarine USS PHILADELPHIA (SSN-690) from behind while she cruised on the surface of the Arabian Gulf. The submarine rolled 40 degrees. Sailors were thrown from their beds. For hours, the vessels sat entangled, drifting toward shallow water, while the crew wondered if they were going to sink. Nobody died. But within days, the Navy fired the captain, the executive officer, and the chief engineer.

Bob Koonce got the call shortly after. At the time, Koonce had just completed an executive officer (second-in-command) tour on a similar ship and had fourteen years of submarine experience. He was sent to rebuild the crew's confidence and get the boat home safely.

"I flew in and found 135 shell-shocked kids," he told me. "Average age twenty-three or twenty-four. They'd just been hit by a freighter. They'd just watched their captain get fired. And most of them loved the guy."

Here's what I've learned from studying incidents like this one. The final accident is not the real failure. That is merely a symptom. The real failure is always the deeper cultural issues that eroded performance and led to the collision.

By some accounts, the culture on the *Philadelphia* wasn't one of high expectations and mutual account-ability. It was fear, avoidance, and going through the motions. By other accounts, the culture was more one of overconfidence. The crew cut corners because they thought they were smarter and better than they were. They did not maintain a questioning attitude. They did not maintain the proper formality.

When that's your culture, the standards and performance will certainly decline. The watch gets less rigorous. Procedures get followed less precisely. Simply put, you do not meet the standards expected of a United States Navy nuclear submarine. And then one night, a freighter will come up behind you in the dark, and nobody sees it.

We tend to think that accountability means responding decisively with discipline when something goes wrong. Although that is a form of accountability, it is *last* line of defense for your standards, not the *first*.

Accountability happens in all the moments *before* a crisis occurs. It happens every time you enforce an expectation, every time you address a shortfall, every time you refuse to accept what you said you wouldn't accept.

Standards are defined by what you tolerate, not what you profess. What you permit defines who you are, and none of that is in your policy manual.

Elite organizations are legendary, almost notorious, for the high expectations they hold their team members to. From NYPD ESU to the US Army Rangers, demanding standards are at the heart of high performance.

In this chapter, I examine what standards are, how they should be set, how they are enforced, and how they form the basis for accountability. We will explore how individual accountability and team accountability interlock, the role of interpersonal accountability in building performance, and the fundamental role of leadership in holding that line.

Trust Is Rooted in Accountability

In tactical units, trust is not a feeling. It's a byproduct of demonstrated competence.

When a SWAT officer makes entry through a door in front of the stack, they trust the teammates behind them to cover their blind spots. They trust the sniper on overwatch to take the shot if needed. They trust the team leader to have planned the operation correctly. This trust is not blind faith. It's earned through repeatedly demonstrated competence verified through objective requirements, and then reinforced through every training evolution, where everyone performed at the level expected.

The same principle certainly applies outside tactical environments. Think about pilots. Before a commercial pilot can take the controls of an aircraft carrying your family, they must meet objective, verifiable requirements. Flight hours. Certifications. Medical clearances. Regular check rides, exams, simulators, recurrent training, and a lot more. You trust the person flying your plane because those requirements have been enforced. You trust the system that tested and licensed that pilot.

What these examples share is that verified competence creates trust. When everyone in a system has been held to the same objective requirements, you can extend trust to people you've never met. You don't need to personally evaluate every pilot, every teammate. The requirements have done that work for you.

Robin Dunbar, the Oxford anthropologist, found that humans can maintain stable social relationships with approximately 150 people. This idea is so powerful it is known as Dunbar's Number. This is why infantry units, Navy ship divisions, aircraft squadrons, departments in computer companies, assembly line units in auto and aircraft manufacturing all have around 150 people. Elite military and law enforcement units tend to contain less than that number.

Below this threshold, peer pressure works effectively, and Dunbar emphasizes that the key is that leaders can *personally* know each person. Above it, you need formal management systems.

Bill Gore, founder of Gore-Tex, deliberately limited his factory sizes to 150 employees for this reason. He observed that at that threshold, "We decided" becomes "they decided." The sense of collective ownership and mutual accountability that characterizes small teams gives way to the anonymity of larger organizations.

In small teams, you know your people. You've seen them perform. Trust is personal. But in larger organizations, or when working with people you've never met, trust becomes systemic. It depends not on personal knowledge but on shared requirements that everyone has met.

That's why demanding requirements and accountability are not in tension with trust. They are the foundation of it. When you join an elite team, you trust your teammates not because you've worked with each of them personally, but because you know they passed the same selection, met the same requirements, and are held to the same accountability you are.

The requirements are the basis for extending trust before it has been personally earned.

> ## HOW TO START:
> ## TRUST IS ROOTED IN ACCOUNTABILITY
>
> List the three most critical performance requirements for your team. Now ask: when did you last verify each one? Not assume, not hope — verify. If you can't answer that question with a specific date and a specific test, you don't have a standard. You have a wish.

Inspected vs. Expected

There's an old saying that goes something like "people do what is inspected, not what is expected." Put more directly, you can have all the expectations in the world, but your team will only pay attention to the ones that you enforce.

Just like with overarching culture, every organization has two sets of standards. The first set hangs on walls, appears in employee handbooks, defines hiring standards, and gets recited at company meetings. These are the *stated values*.

The second set shows up in who gets promoted, what behavior gets corrected, what gets quietly overlooked, and how leaders spend their efforts. These are the *actual values*.

Although these two sets of standards will always vary slightly, to have an elite organization there must be very little room between what you expect and what you inspect. When there is wide divergence between the two, employees quickly learn that words don't matter, that only actions do. In other words, they do not need to completely meet the standards of the organization so long as they pay attention to the things that other people get punished for and just avoid the same mistakes. This will completely undermine the performance of the organization little by little by eroding its foundation.

If you want to have high performance, you must have high standards, and everyone in the organization must adhere to them.

It is essential that your standards are seamlessly integrated into your organizational culture. Everyone follows the standards, the standards are spoken about openly, and the cultural expectations are clear. When this is the case, there is silent culture pressure to adhere to standards.

Tennis legend Billie Jean King once reportedly said, "Pressure is a privilege." When your organization holds you to high standards, and there are consequences for falling short, you feel the weight of expectations. Not as punishment but as respect. Pressure means that someone believes you're capable of meeting those standards. It means you're part of something that matters enough to have requirements worth enforcing.

Leaders often fear that high expectations will drive away their best performers, but the opposite is true. Knives need, and want, to be sharpened. They don't want a wooden spoon culture. They want an environment that demands their best.

People don't grow in the absence of challenge. They coast. And coasting organizations don't stay in business, don't win championships, and don't save lives when freighters hit them in the middle of the night.

Without clear expectations, organizations decline. Not suddenly, but gradually. The watch gets a little less rigorous. The paperwork gets a little sloppier. The edge gets a little duller. By the time anyone notices, you've redefined your culture. You've become an organization that accepts mediocrity, and your performance has become substandard.

HOW TO START:
INSPECTING, NOT EXPECTING

Write down your top ten key expectations for your team. Circle the ones you actively measure or enforce. The uncircled items are wishes, not standards. What do you expect but consistently don't get?

Accountability Is a Three-Way Street

For the majority of organizations, accountability is a one-way street that flows downward. Leaders hold their teams accountable. Managers monitor direct reports. Supervisors correct subordinates.

But in truly healthy organizations, particularly in elite teams, accountability runs in three directions: up, down, and sideways.

Downward accountability is the most familiar and obvious. Leaders set expectations, monitor performance, and address shortfalls. This is essential, and without it standards exist in name only. Someone has to be responsible for enforcement, and in most organizational structures, that someone is the leader. When downward accountability fails, you get the *Philadelphia,* where leadership allowed declining performance until a catastrophe forced correction.

Upward accountability is less common in organizations. This is the team's ability to hold leadership accountable. In dysfunctional organizations, this accountability doesn't exist. Leaders are exempt from the requirements they enforce on others. They arrive late but penalize lateness in others. They demand transparency but operate in secrecy and preach values they don't practice themselves. Upward accountability means leaders must be held to the same or higher bar as everyone else.

When a leader violates a standard or fails to follow through on their responsibilities, it is essential that the team has both the permission and the responsibility to call them on it. This of course requires that leaders are open to this and make it clear to their team that they want to be held to organizational standards.

In tactical units this might be leadership showing up for PT and firearms qualifications and demonstrably meeting standards. Whereas in a corporate environment, it could be leaders showing up on time for meetings, following through on deadlines, and conspicuously following the rules that others are expected to follow. No matter what the case, to have upward accountability leaders should explicitly give permission to those they lead to hold them accountable.

The final form of accountability is lateral or peer-to-peer accountability. This is where teammates hold each other accountable constantly without waiting for a supervisor to intervene.

In tactical units, lateral accountability frequently takes the form of joking, off-color comments, and nicknames. A teammate who is slipping or falling behind might find themselves the target of pointed humor or chats over drinks long before any supervisor gets involved. In other more serious cases, this might escalate to a formal sit-down and more direct conversations between teammates.

In high-performing teams, this is often the most powerful form of accountability. We usually care more about the judgment of our peers than the judgment of our bosses, and the social reward system makes us want to belong to the group. Of course, in all social situations, belonging to a group means meeting the group's expectations. So whether you are running a SWAT team or a kids' soccer team, peer-to-peer accountability always has a profound effect on the team.

It is important to say that all forms of accountability demand clear standards and expectations that are applicable to everyone. They also demand a clear cultural understanding that accountability is an act of caring.

HOW TO START: DRIVING THE 3-WAY STREET

When was the last time someone on your level held you accountable? How about someone below you? If you can't remember either, you have a hierarchy, not collaboration. Give people permission to challenge you.

Accountability That Fits the Group

Of course, personal accountability won't look the same in every organization. What is socially acceptable in a tactical unit won't work in a law office. What you see on an NFL sideline certainly won't translate to an elementary school. So it is essential that accountability mechanisms fit into the culture and accountability mechanisms adjust to the appropriate level by population.

During the 2024 Super Bowl, Travis Kelce lost his temper with how the game was going. He yelled at his head coach Andy Reid and then physically shoved him on live television. The media clutched their pearls and news commentators wondered why Kelce wasn't benched or suspended.

Yet Coach Reid barely reacted. Why? Because cultural boundaries regulate behavior, and Coach Reid was perfectly okay being challenged by his players.

Professional football players live in a world of extreme physical violence and train with constant physical contact. Hugging, slapping, shoving, bumping, and yelling are all perfectly socially acceptable in their world. While Kelce's behavior certainly would have been unacceptable in an office environment, it was only slightly past the line in the NFL.

As a result, Reid didn't bench Kelce. He didn't publicly dress him down, and he didn't freak out. He grabbed his arm, stayed calm, and kept one of his best players on the field and engaged in the game.

Did they have a private conversation later? Oh yeah, I am sure they did. But I am also sure there was not an HR complaint filed by Reid.

The lesson here is that accountability takes many forms, and the form must fit the culture. Holding others accountable is essential, but it is also essential that the format of that accountability fits the social boundaries of the organization and not to create a bullying environment. Everyone has to feel safe, and departing from social boundaries needs to be prevented.

Although making a teammate run laps or do burpees when they are late to a training session is totally fine in a tactical unit, that is not the case for a preschool teacher who is late to work.

In each environment it is essential that we mold the accountability to the people in the group. I have different accountability conversations with my salespeople and warehouse team than I do with my accounting and purchasing teams.

In all cases, accountability must flow in all three directions. If it only flows down, you have compliance, not commitment. And compliance is a fragile foundation for excellence.

HOW TO START: ACCOUNTABILITY THAT FITS THE GROUP

Think about the last time you held someone accountable for a performance issue. Was the approach calibrated to your culture, or did you apply a one-size-fits-all response? Different people, different teams, and different environments require different approaches. Is your accountability style actually landing or is it either too soft to register or too harsh to feel fair?

Leadership Is Gardening

General Stanley McChrystal commanded Joint Special Operations Command, or JSOC, the most elite special operations force in American military history: Delta Force, SEAL Team Six, and smaller specialized units from the Air Force and Army. Despite having superior technology, training, and firepower, his forces were struggling against Al-Qaeda in Iraq. The enemy was decentralized, adaptive, and fast. McChrystal's hierarchical command structure, optimized for efficiency, simply couldn't keep pace.

The transformation that followed forever changed how he understood leadership itself and viewed himself. McChrystal, who himself came from a career in these specialized units, describes this shift as moving from being a "chess master" to seeing himself as a "gardener." The chess master controls every piece, dictates every move, maintains central command. The gardener does something different entirely.

The gardener creates conditions for growth: the right soil, adequate water, proper sunlight. But the gardener cannot force the plants to grow. That has to happen on its own.

Your job is to create conditions where people can excel. Set the expectations. Build the culture. Provide the resources. Then step back and let them perform. You maintain visibility into operations, you understand what's happening, you're present and available.

But you resist the urge to intervene constantly, trusting empowered teams to execute.

What makes the gardening metaphor even more complete is that gardening isn't just about nurturing growth. It's also about defending the garden. Protecting it from disease. Keeping out the pests. Resisting the urge to plant more than the soil can support. Perhaps most importantly, knowing when to trim the branches to protect the plant or help its growth. A gardener who only waters and never defends will soon have a garden overrun with nasty creatures that shouldn't be there.

Michael Lumpkin learned this lesson in the most demanding circumstances imaginable. Lumpkin was a Navy SEAL Captain who would eventually rise to become the Assistant Secretary of Defense for Special Operations and Low-Intensity Conflict. But when September 11 happened, he was running training for all West Coast SEAL teams. What followed was unprecedented pressure to expand special operations forces as fast as possible.

The scale was staggering. The special operations community grew from roughly 33,000 people to over 50,000. For the SEAL teams specifically, the Navy created two new teams in a matter of years. On the West Coast alone, they went from three SEAL teams to four. That's 25 percent more SEALs in a culture in which it takes years to make a single SEAL.

"When you grow something quickly," Lumpkin told me, "there's a real risk of dilution and capability. Frequently you're sacrificing capability with numbers."

The pressure came from above. The nation was at war, our military commanders needed more SEAL operators, and the politicians wanted results. The easiest path would have been to lower the standards, to get more bodies through training, and to meet the demand. That's what most organizations do when growth pressure hits.

Lumpkin refused.

Instead, he made a counterintuitive decision: He pulled his best operators out of the fight and put them in training.

This is the opposite of what most organizations do. The typical pattern, in both military and law enforcement, is to staff training with whomever you can spare. The best and brightest stay on the front lines. The training cadre gets the leftovers.

But Lumpkin understood something important: The whole point is to make *many* best and bright people. You can only do that if your trainers are the model you want to replicate.

He also instituted rigorous inspection. Lumpkin explained, crediting Admiral Hyman Rickover and the submarine force culture. "As a leader, you have to make sure that you are the keeper of the standards.

You have to do inspections. Gear inspections is one thing, but there's also inspecting the tactics, making sure they make sense, that they will bring everybody home, that they will accomplish the mission. It's a tireless and never-ending job, but you have to do it or you will be unsatisfied with the outcomes. And especially in life-and-death situations, people will die."

The warning Lumpkin offers is about how expectations erode. It doesn't happen all at once. It happens incrementally. "Once you do get complacent, you set a new baseline, and it happens over time. It happens over and over and over again, and pretty soon you're somewhere where you don't want to be."

He saw this play out even in the SEAL teams during the height of the Iraq and Afghanistan conflicts. Some teams were so focused on the current fight that they stopped doing combat swimmer operations entirely. Think about that: SEALs who weren't diving. They had neglected one of the basic competencies that defines who they are because the operational tempo pushed everything else aside.

"You have to make sure that you do it," Lumpkin said. "It's hard. It's difficult to put ten pounds of stuff into a five-pound bag, but you have to spend the time to do it. You have to train and prepare for the worst possible circumstance. Prepare for the worst and hope for the best. It's not the other way around."

That's what it means to be a gardener. Not just nurturing growth, but actively defending the conditions that make growth possible. Defending against external pressure to expand faster than quality allows. Defending against the gradual drift that happens when inspection lapses. Defending against the temptation to staff training with your second string while keeping your best people in the fight.

You are the keeper of the standards. That's your job. And keeping standards requires constant vigilance, active inspection, and the courage to resist the pressures that would otherwise compromise what you've built.

The leader who won't defend the garden will eventually have no garden left worth tending.

HOW TO START: BEING A BETTER GARDENER

Name one thing you've planted, one weed you pulled, and one thing you've neglected in the last 90 days. Are you planting and weeding or neglecting?

KEY PRINCIPLES

- Verified competence creates trust. People extend trust to systems that enforce consistent, objective standards — not to personalities.
- People do what is inspected, not what is expected. You are the keeper of the standards. If you don't check, it doesn't count.
- Accountability flows three ways: up, down, and sideways.
- Accountability must fit the culture. The format must match the social boundaries of the organization. One size does not fit all.
- Your job is to create conditions for growth, not to control every outcome. Be the gardener, not the chess master.

What Comes Next

High expectations create accountability. But accountability without collaboration is just compliance. People will meet the minimum requirement to avoid consequences, but they won't bring their best thinking, their creative energy, their collective wisdom. The next chapter explores how elite teams harvest collective wisdom through deliberate collaboration, turning individual excellence into something greater than the sum of its parts.

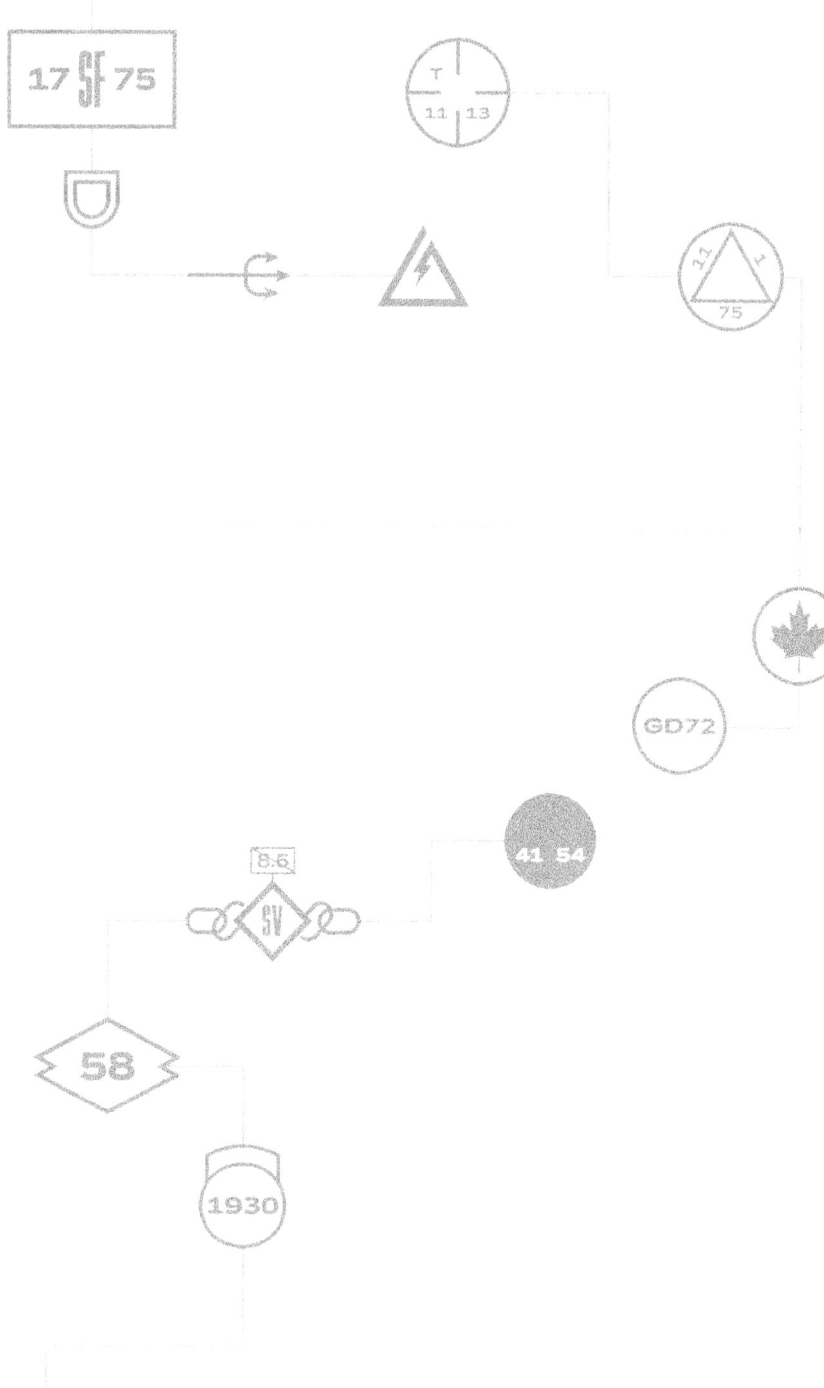

CHAPTER SIX

COLLABORATE DELIBERATELY

Thank You For Disagreeing

The catalog was ready to go to press. Thousands of copies of our annual product guide were about to be printed. Weeks of prep work by a team of experienced professionals to ensure it was perfect. Multiple rounds of review. Everyone had signed off.

On a whim, I grabbed a proof copy and walked it over to our warehouse. One of our guys there had been with us for maybe six months. I handed it to him as a final sanity check. Do me a favor and just read this and look for anything that seems out of place or wrong. I was not really expecting him to find anything. He glanced at the cover, looked up, and said, "Is this a joke? Did you intentionally spell the company name wrong?"

Right there on the front cover, the company name AARDVARK was spelled AAARDVARK. We had all proofed this catalog and done weeks of review, yet somehow we didn't see that the company name was misspelled. And this guy caught it in thirty seconds?

Fortunately, we were able to fix it before it went to press because someone with fresh eyes looked at it and caught the error. But if I had not walked over to the warehouse, if I had assumed we had it covered, we would have printed and mailed thousands of catalogs with our company name spelled wrong right on the cover.

At our next company-wide meeting, I stood up with that proof copy and told the story. I told our team that the "experts," including me as the CEO, had failed a basic recheck that our teammate in the warehouse caught in thirty seconds. I publicly thanked him for saving us from ourselves. I wanted everyone to see that, in this organization, the truth carries more rank than the person telling it. If you save the company from a disaster, I do not care how long you have been here or what your role is, you are a hero.

That moment crystallized something for me that I had been observing for years in elite tactical units. The smartest person in the room is never one person. It is the room itself. The warehouse guy was not smarter than our marketing team. He simply had fresh eyes, a different perspective, no assumptions about what the cover was supposed to look like. He saw what was actually there, instead of what he expected to see.

As I have discussed, all organizations are just the sum of the people in that organization. The success of the organization is just the collective efforts of their people. Good teams are certainly made up of good people, but collaboration is how those good people become a team to do something great. But the organization must be able to harvest the skills and wisdom of the people it employs.

In the previous chapter, I examined how high standards create accountability. Yet, how accountability without collaboration will yield only compliance. People follow rules without contributing ideas. They execute plans without improving them.

Standards tell you what to do. Collaboration is the vehicle through which you can accomplish your mission. Elite teams don't just work together; they create an environment where the best idea wins regardless of source. They build cultures where questioning is expected and where collective intelligence is harnessed.

This chapter explores five methods for harvesting that collective intelligence. The thread connecting them is simple. To take advantage of the wisdom of the crowd, we need to get to ground truth, remove rank from planning, and attack our own ideas before reality does. None of these practices require special technology. All of them require leaders who are willing to learn from those they lead and listen to things they might not want to hear.

The Wisdom of the Crowd

The New York City Police Department has a unit called the Emergency Service Unit. ESU is often described as 911 for NYPD. ESU houses one of the broadest skill sets of any tactical unit in the world, ranging from hostage rescue to counter-terror missions, from high angle to water rescue, and from urban search and rescue to tactical paramedic services. When NYPD officers have a problem they can't solve, ESU is their first phone call.

Because of this broad mission set, however, it is impossible for any one ESU operator to be exceptional at everything. So everyone is trained across the board on the required general skills, and then individual team members are encouraged (that is, expected) to deepen their expertise in different specialty areas.

Joe Bucchignano spent twenty years at ESU. When I interviewed him on *The Debrief*, one of the most unique aspects of ESU that he talked about was their approach to intentionally selecting diverse people and then deferring to their expertise. This is not diverse from a DEI perspective, but rather diverse from a life experience and training standpoint.

Their goal is to always harvest all the skills they can from whoever ends up on a call. Then, like building a LEGO set made up of different pieces, assemble the best team they can for the mission at hand.

As Bucchignano put it, their selection looks for people who bring a special skill set to the table. It could be something silly like being a certified locksmith or working at a bird rescue. Or it can be something directly transferable like being an EMT, a volunteer firefighter, or a military background. In any case, teammates are bringing something to the unit that the unit can now utilize and benefit from.

ESU's interoperability model recognizes two levels of expertise: shared fundamentals that everyone possesses, and local expertise that varies by assignment or person. All ESU officers share foundational training. But Truck One handles more subway rescues, Truck Three handles different terrain, Staten Island deals with deer, and so on.

The cultural norm is explicit deference to local expertise regardless of seniority. As Bucchignano said, "I don't care if I've been here for ten years and you've been here for three. I'm going to just let you run with this because you've experienced this before and I definitely have not."

This requires humility and a culture that doesn't equate seniority with omniscience, but it also allows

ESU to harvest the highest possible performance from each subunit.

Ed Catmull stated this elegantly: "Give a good idea to a mediocre team and they will screw it up. Give a mediocre idea to a good team and they will make it better, or they will throw it away and come up with something that works." The goal is not to find the genius with the perfect idea; it is to build a team that can iterate any idea toward excellence.

When Catmull was asked to lead Walt Disney Animation, a studio several times larger than Pixar, he replicated this system. The results were remarkable. With zero staff turnover, Disney began generating hits again. The people had not changed. The process had. The same professionals who had been struggling suddenly became successful because they had a system for capturing collective intelligence.

There is also a paradox to expertise. The more experienced you are, the more likely you are to see what you expect rather than what exists. The catalog reviewers I discussed previously knew the company name so well, they could not see it misspelled. Their expertise became a blind spot, because the pattern recognition that makes experts valuable also makes them vulnerable to missing what a novice would catch immediately.

I have seen this pattern repeatedly across hundreds of tactical teams. The commander who has executed a hundred operations stops questioning whether this operation should be executed the same way. The veteran detective who has worked dozens of cases stops noticing details that would jump out at a rookie. Expertise creates assumptions, and assumptions create blind spots.

Elite teams understand this. They build systems to harvest perspectives from everyone, not just the senior people, not just the subject-matter experts, and not just the voices that usually get heard.

They create environments where the warehouse guy feels comfortable pointing out the obvious and where the newest member of the team can challenge the plan. More importantly, where disagreement is welcomed rather than suppressed.

Mark McGrath, who has spent decades studying John Boyd's work on decision-making, explains the mechanism of why this works. Different people bring different orientations shaped by their unique experiences and mental models.

"If we look different but we all think alike," McGrath notes, "that is not real diversity. If we look different, we think different, we see the world differently, that diversity is unstoppable." You do not need smarter people. You need more perspectives.

The wisdom is not in any individual. It is in the room.

> ## HOW TO START:
> ## HARVESTING YOUR RESOURCES
>
> Map your last three significant decisions. Who contributed to the decision and research? Was it always the same small group? If so, you're not using your team's collective intelligence. Expand the circle.

Get to Ground Truth

As you move up in an organization, people naturally want to please you. They bring you the wins, the high margins, the happy clients. But they also want to hide the missed deadlines, the toxic teammates, the failing projects. They tell themselves they are "managing" the situation or "protecting" your time, but they are, in truth, starving the operating system of the data it needs to survive. If you only sit in your office, you will eventually lose orientation over what is happening at ground level and get hit by something you never saw coming.

To harvest the wisdom of your team, it is essential that you leave the office and go hunt for bad news yourself. The military calls this concept the ground truth. In other words, find out what is happening on the ground where the battle is taking place.

After Phil Hansen retired from LASD-SEB he became the chief of police for the city of Santa Maria, California. As the chief, Hansen used to ensure that he regularly visited every shift's daily briefing, including graveyard shift. The chief of police, showing up at two in the morning just to see his personnel face to face, was an unusual practice. But it gave him the opportunity to see them and ask: How are things? What is going on? What are we missing?

Hansen understood that people's perspectives are always skewed by their personal interests and passions, and that it's nearly impossible to develop trust from people who never see your face nor is it possible to know what is really going on. The truth your key staff thinks they see may not always be the team's truth. In fact, it frequently is not.

Every layer of hierarchy between you and the ground adds filtering. The better your direct reports are, the more accurate your ground truth. But it is never completely accurate. The only way to get unfiltered information is to go where the work happens.

Pete Blaber, the former Delta Force Commander, built his leadership philosophy around "the guy on the ground" principle. The person closest to the problem almost always has the best information about it. The challenge is creating systems that capture that information before decisions get made.

Chief John Perez of Pasadena PD adopted this strategy when he took over as chief. In a city with a strong anti-police advocacy community, and a historically contentious relationship with them, Perez viewed his critics as a source of ground truth and embraced them. In fact, he invited activists who wanted to defund the police to serve on his advisory board. "If your advisory council only contains supporters, it provides no value," he explains. "I needed people that were going to criticize me." The criticism made every decision better.

One caveat to ground truth is worth mentioning: You must always respect the trust of those who tell you the unvarnished truth. Sharing ground truth places the person who shares it in peril. As a result, you can never burn your source. When someone tells you something actionable, you may have to wait to act on it until there is a way that is not attributable to the source, which can be frustrating. But getting the truth means respecting the source.

HOW TO START: HUNTING GROUND TRUTH

Spend time this week where the actual work happens in your organization. Don't schedule a visit, show up unannounced, ask questions, and listen more than you talk. Give people permission to speak truthfully.

Rank-Off Planning

In tactical operations, a flawed plan can get people killed. The stakes are too high for politeness, or deference to seniority, or protecting the boss's ego. That is why most elite units utilize rank-off planning sessions. During planning sessions, rank is disregarded ("comes off") and all team members are treated as equals regardless of position or seniority. Everyone has a voice at the table and everyone's opinion matters. No one is too junior to challenge ideas or add to the discussion. Nor is anyone seen as so important that their opinion carries undue weight. The goal is to harness the entire group's wisdom by giving everyone a chance to speak, ask questions, propose solutions or challenge ideas.

The result is a candid, open planning discussion where ideas are discussed and challenged based on the merit of the ideas and not based on the importance of who originally came up with the idea. Everyone's ideas are evaluated with the express goal of finding the "best plan" through group discussion and debate.

A common approach to these sessions is having members speak in reverse seniority order meaning that the junior members speak first. This allows everyone to speak before the most senior members do which prevents them from skewing the discussion. After all, it is much easier to state that you like a certain approach BEFORE the CEO says he likes a different approach.

The goal is to harvest the entire wisdom and experience of the group by removing any obstacles to candid discussion. Then, once a draft plan is determined, the entire plan is attacked, by everyone, to identify its potential points of failure and weaknesses. Once the plan is finalized, then rank "goes back on" and the team returns to normal operations to implement the plan.

This overt admission of fallibility by leadership has an exceptional effect on the culture of groups. Leaders who run rank-off planning sessions implicitly say "I care more about getting this right than I do about my ego." This is a powerful message.

Implementing this in the corporate world works just like it does in tactical units. Rank, position, and seniority are "overtly removed" for discussions by leadership. Leadership explicitly lays the ground rules for the discussion affirming that everyone's opinion matters and that everyone has a voice at the table. They then ensure that everyone uses that voice by prompting discussion, encouraging participation and modeling the correct behaviors for the discussion. This is a process and it won't work the first time. It will require repeated attempts and cultural affirmation to take hold. But once it does, the quality of decisions will improve dramatically.

One important distinction is that this is not decision by committee. One of my favorite sayings is that a camel is a racehorse designed by committee. The goal is not to reach a compromise or settlement where everyone is happy. Consensus decision-making is the worst possible way to make decisions. Making everyone happy means making no one truly happy and what starts out as a process to design a Kentucky Derby winner ends up creating a camel that doesn't even come close to the intended purpose.

The idea here is to take everyone's input, stress-test ideas through rigorous argument, and then let leadership finalize the plan once the process stops yielding results. We are not taking the average of all the ideas or splitting the difference and compromising on everything.

Once a plan has been finalized, then rank goes back on, team structure is reestablished, and leadership picks a final solution. This egalitarian process is for planning only. Execution still requires clear lines of authority and unity of command.

Importantly, once the planning cycle and time for disagreement has ended, everyone must be expected to get behind the decision and support it. The time for debate ends when the decision is made. No one gets the luxury of complaining about the plan once the decision is made. Nor is it culturally acceptable to undermine the decision because you disagreed with it. This kind of behavior destroys the entire collaborative process and undermines group cohesion.

> ## HOW TO START: RUN A RANK-OFF SESSION
>
> Before your next planning meeting, state the rules for the session out loud. Rank comes off, junior staff speak first, and every idea is evaluated on merit not source. If your idea still always wins, the rank never really came off.

Murder Your Own Ideas

In 1987 Mike Tyson was asked about his upcoming fight with Tyrell Biggs, who claimed to have a plan to beat him. Tyson uttered perhaps his most eloquent line ever: "Everybody has plans until they get hit for the first time."

Truer words were never spoken about planning no matter whether you run a tactical operation, are a Fortune 500 CEO, or run a doggie daycare center. Plans are always made in a vacuum, and even if done collaboratively they have a way of coming undone when they make contact with the real world.

The way that elite tactical units prepare for this is by red teaming. This idea originated in tactical training. The way it works is that a group of neutral, objective people (who were not part of the planning) are brought in to serve as an opposing force, or a red team, during training exercises. The red team's objective is to defeat your team (blue team) to expose the weaknesses of the team or its plans. This can take the form of physically defeating in tactical force-on-force training or academically defeating them in a table-top exercise.

In either case, the goal of red teaming is the same: Expose weaknesses before an actual operation through the adversarial process.

This practice can be applied to any decision-making process and goes way beyond just playing devil's advocate—it is full-scale intellectual combat aimed at exposing every weakness. Hence the "Murder Your Ideas" heading here.

By attacking our own strategies, we test their vulnerabilities. When weaknesses are exposed, they are immediately addressed.

For us to accomplish this in the corporate world, we must build systems that allow us to attack our own ideas constructively. We need to promote a culture where the goal isn't for any individual to be right, but for the team to collectively find the best solution. Which of course means setting aside ego, embracing disagreement, and allowing others to improve the ideas.

The organizational mindset has to be that getting the right answer to a problem is far more important than anyone's ego. There has to be a universal understanding that no idea is born perfect and that by attacking it and exposing its weaknesses we will always make it better. Planning is iteration and criticism is support.

Think back to the Pixar Brain Trust, in the words of Ed Catmull: "Every creative project necessarily starts as a disaster." Teams never get the right ideas immediately. The magic happens in the iteration, in the process of making bad ideas better through collective intelligence.

Marc Polymeropoulos, a former senior CIA operations officer who ran clandestine operations in some of the most dangerous environments on earth, describes how his team always had someone assigned to act as an in-house red team, which he calls the process monkey. The process monkey asks: Have we checked all our boxes, the very essential basics, to ensure success? And then, have we considered all the angles? What are we missing? Who has not been heard from? What assumptions might be wrong? Their job is to murder bad ideas before those ideas murder the mission.

Ironically, in most organizations, this person is seen as an obstacle. As someone who is just stopping progress or getting in the way. Yet, in elite organizations, they are recognized as an essential part of the process.

This natural tension is essential for any team that wants to achieve elite performance. We must build red teaming into our planning processes.

Perhaps more importantly, we must always reinforce the value of this process to our team and help others to understand why this tension is critical to our success. As leaders we must model humility and gratitude to those who are willing to attack our plans. When the boss's plan gets attacked, everyone watches. If the response is defensive, red teaming dies. If the response is genuine consideration, flexibility and gratitude red teaming will thrive.

No matter how well you plan, your plan will ultimately be executed in the real world with opponents trying to defeat it and unpredictable variables getting in the way. If you don't murder your own plans ahead of time to reduce the potential failure points the real world may murder them at a very inconvenient time.

HOW TO START: RED TEAMING

Before finalizing your next significant plan, assign two people who weren't involved in the planning to attack it. Ask them to find every weakness and every way it fails. Then thank the Red Team publicly and fix what they identified.

Everybody Hates Surprises

To maintain a collaborative environment, it is also essential that the organization feel predictable. This doesn't mean it has to be static, constant, or even stable, but it needs to be predictable. Predictability creates a sense of safety in the team and encourages people to take risks and challenge thinking.

Of course, no matter how well you run an organization, periodically you will be required to change direction and sometimes this will be significant. The challenge is how to change direction without breaking team collaboration or trust.

Bill Kirst, the host of the *Coffee and Change* podcast, has been a corporate change leader for some of the largest tech companies in the world. Kirst's job is helping large organizations adapt to change. He explains change in a way that changed my perspective on it: "When we face change, it's essentially a mini-episode of grief." We are grieving what used to be, which is true even if we agree with the change. Obviously that grief is worse if we do not agree with it.

Change undermines our sense of control over our world—and to some degree our trust in the organization. Thus, to ensure collaboration, it is essential that leaders make change as predictable as possible and give the team members a sense of ownership over changes.

One way to accomplish this is to socialize your changes and gather feedback from members of the team. In small teams this may mean the team helping to figure out the course of action. In larger organizations it may simply mean explaining the rationale for your decisions. But always the goal is to minimize disruption to collaboration.

People can accept decisions they disagree with, as long as they feel the process was fair. What they cannot accept is being blindsided, being told what to do without understanding why, or having the rules change without warning. Fair process builds trust even when outcomes are not what people wanted. Unfair process destroys trust even when the outcome would have been acceptable.

HOW TO START: BEING PREDICTABLE

When was the last time your team was caught off guard by a decision or change they should have known about? Each surprise represents a broken communication channel. Socialize before you announce.

KEY PRINCIPLES

- Psychological safety is the foundation: People must feel safe to speak up.
- Junior speaks first—hierarchy anchors discussion and silences good ideas.
- Get to ground truth: The map is not the territory.
- Murder your own ideas before the enemy does.
- The wisdom of the crowd requires equal voice, not loudest voice.

What Comes Next

Collaboration generates options. But options without decisions create paralysis. The diversity that makes teams wise can also make them slow. At some point, the talking must stop and someone must decide. The next chapter examines how elite teams build decision machines: systems that convert collective wisdom into decisive action when time is short, information is incomplete, and the stakes are high.

Collaboration without decision authority is just a conversation. Decision authority without collaboration is just a gamble.

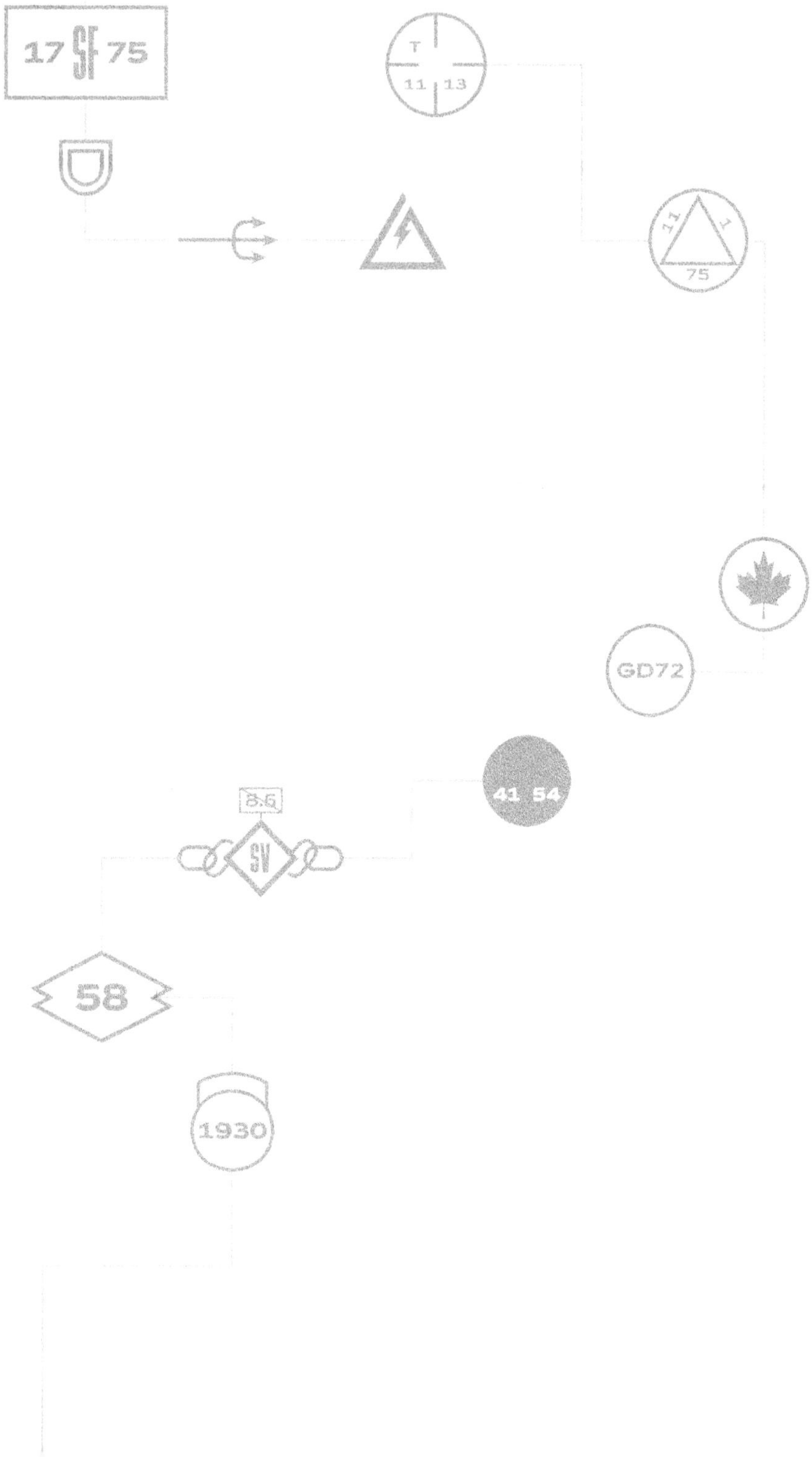
17 SF 75
T
11 13
11 1
75
GD72
41 54
8.6
SV
58
1930

CHAPTER SEVEN

BUILD A DECISION MACHINE

*Make a F*cking Decision*

It was a Monday morning in December 2014, the week before Christmas, when a lone gunman walked into a Lindt chocolate café in the heart of Sydney, Australia, with a shotgun and a purported improvised explosive device (IED). Within minutes, he had taken eighteen hostages. Within hours, the entire nation was watching. Within sixteen hours, two innocent people would be dead.

The Lindt Café was located at Martin Place in Sydney's financial district, directly across the street from one of Australia's largest television stations. The gunman could not have chosen a more visible location from which to terrorize the city. As news helicopters circled overhead and cameras broadcast every moment live, one of Australia's most elite tactical units took up position just meters from the café's front door.

The New South Wales Tactical Operations Unit (TOU) was highly trained, well-equipped, and had developed a solid tactical plan. They were prepared for this type of event. But, sadly, for the next sixteen hours they waited to get permission to execute it.

Ben Bessant was the entry team leader for the Alpha team on that day. A former soldier who had become a police tactical officer, Bessant had spent years training for exactly this kind of moment. As the hours dragged on and the situation inside the café deteriorated, Bessant and his teammates grew increasingly alarmed.

Not at the terrorist, but at the silence from their own command structure. The team wanted to execute a deliberate action (DA) entry to rescue the hostages, but the senior leadership on scene refused. Although there was no clear reason articulated, it is safe to assume that the combination of an IED threat and that no hostages were currently being harmed certainly created a reason to not take action.

From the team's perspective, a deliberate action would have allowed them to enter on their own terms, using their training, their tactics, and the element of surprise. Instead, they were told to wait, thus allowing the gunman to dictate the timeline.

The team's frustration mounted as every indicator pointed toward catastrophe. The gunman refused to speak directly with negotiators. His demands were all rejected.

Seven hours in, hostages began escaping on their own, a desperate act that signaled the situation was spiraling. To the tactical operators on the street, each escape was a warning sign that the gunman was losing his grip, and a cornered, tired, panicking terrorist is dangerous and unpredictable.

But to the commanders in the command post, the escapes meant something else entirely, as Bessant said: "From what we heard back from upper management, they didn't seem to see it that way at all. Making no decision and sitting it out has resulted in hostages escaping and he hasn't actually executed anyone yet. So speculation says they were probably happy with how things were progressing."

This is the trap of decision inertia. Since nothing catastrophic had happened yet, and there was a reason to not take action, leadership interpreted their inaction as success. The absence of disaster became evidence that the current course was working. Every hour that passed without violence made it harder to justify action, even as every hour brought them closer to exactly that outcome.

Meanwhile, the tactical team did everything they could to force a decision. They submitted their deliberate action plan. When it was rejected, they coordinated with Australia's military special forces commandos, who built a mock-up of the café, rehearsed the police team's plan, and reported back that it was tactically sound.

The answer from command remained unchanged. "At no point during the day did they ever approve a DA plan," Bessant said when I interviewed him. "The only permission we were given throughout the day was only to react upon him basically executing a hostage or a hostage being in risk of serious harm."

As night fell and the siege stretched past midnight, the breaking point finally came. Just after 2:00 a.m., six more hostages made a desperate break for the door. The gunman opened fire, blasting out a glass panel just above their heads as they fled. The tactical team surged to full readiness.

"We were completely heightened at that point. He's now tried to fire on hostages and kill them. So we stood ready for deployment. I was second in the stack, physically pressed against Paulie in front of me, M4 up. Completely ready. It just had to happen there. Had to finally happen."

And then: nothing.

Bessant said, "We were just waiting for that code word and it never happened. And then minutes went past. As you can imagine, the frustration within our team, and we still just weren't allowed to deploy."

The gunman, enraged by the escaping hostages, grabbed the café manager, a man named Tori Johnson who had refused to leave as long as any of his customers remained inside. Johnson had spent the entire siege protecting others, positioning himself between the gunman and the more vulnerable hostages. Now the gunman forced him to his knees, pressed a shotgun to the back of his head, and pulled the trigger.

Only then did the authorization come: "Tiger-tiger-tiger."

The team executed their emergency action, breaching the café and killing the gunman in seconds. But it was too late for Tori Johnson.

And, in the chaos of the entry, another hostage, a young lawyer named Katrina Dawson, was fatally wounded by fragments from police gunfire.

Ben Bessant carries the weight of that night with him: "To this day it's still difficult for me to talk about, purely because we weren't allowed to do our job, what we should have done, and that was to go in and contain the threat that ultimately killed him before he managed to execute a hostage. And if my team and I had been allowed to do that, I believe he'd still be alive today. We're trained to a very high level to deal with this situation. And at no point were we actually allowed to do our job."

The coroner's inquest would later deliver a scathing assessment of the command structure's failure to authorize the tactical team's plan.

Lindt Café has become a case study in the catastrophic cost of indecision. It is also a graphic illustration for any organization about the need to build an effective decision-making machine at the center of their culture. Decision lag is a tax on momentum. It doesn't just delay results; it rots them from the inside and drives your best people to the exit.

This chapter is about building a decision machine so that not deciding never becomes your default decision. We will consider how to achieve situational awareness, utilize the organization's wisdom to choose the correct course of action, push decision-making to the appropriate level, assess risk, and learn from prior decisions.

Make a F*cking Decision

In the song "Freewill" the legendary rock band Rush argues that choosing not to make a decision is actually still making a decision. This single line has become kind of a mantra for decision-making when I teach leadership to tactical units.

Making decisions is difficult and, as a result, many leaders have lost, or more accurately given up, their ability to make decisions. This is not a course of action that will lead to elite performance. Lindt Café is by no means the exception to the rule in modern leadership. We have reached epidemic levels of decision avoidance.

This is largely because we are incentivizing the wrong behaviors in our leaders. Generally, leaders are punished much more harshly for decisions they make than they are for decisions they avoid.

In fact, it is actually very rare that people are punished for failing to make decisions. As a result, leaders have started to realize that not deciding is often the safest option. But choosing not to decide is choosing to surrender control to fate. This simply cannot be allowed in your team if you want good performance.

Many years ago, I was with a friend who ran a high-profile military unit that did a lot of covert work. We were discussing decision-making so I asked him what his rules were for making decisions.

He gave me a wry smile and said, "I have only one rule for decision-making: make a fucking decision."

He went on to explain that the reason he has this rule is that as the consequences of decision rise, it is easy to get bogged down in trying to get perfect information before making a choice. The search for information then becomes an excuse to not make a decision, which in turn takes them into the decision trap: Eventually you will wait long enough that there is no decision to make.

Elite teams do not outsource outcomes to fate. In elite units leaders are expected to make decisions. They are also expected to periodically make mistakes. But elite teams realize that failing to make a decision will always lead to a worse outcome than occasionally making the wrong decision will. So they have created a cultural bias toward decision-making and are willing to accept the risks inherent.

This approach, if adopted into your culture, will dramatically improve the performance of your team. But the culture of the organization must develop this bias toward decision-making in individual leaders.

As General Jim Mattis notes in his book *Call Sign Chaos*, "Instillation of personal initiative, aggressiveness, and risk-taking doesn't spring forward spontaneously on the battlefield. It must be cultivated for years and inculcated, even rewarded, in an organization's culture."

To create a culture of decision-makers, the leadership must have the compassion to accept imperfect outcomes and the commitment to support their people even when they are wrong. This is true for you as an individual as well. You must give yourself permission to make mistakes.

Think about it this way, there is no way to know if your decision is correct at the time you make it. A decision without risk of error is not a decision, it's obvious.

Every decision you make is a hypothesis about what you think will happen. Every decision has risk. If you make enough decisions, there is a 100 percent chance you will make the wrong choice at some point.

Embrace that. Give yourself permission to make mistakes. While this seems terrifying, you will soon realize it is actually liberating. Too often we are afraid to be wrong. But being wrong is part of the process, you will never be perfect.

The same is true when you lead decision makers. We should not judge decision-makers on outcomes they cannot control. Doing so causes them to seek perfect decisions, which require perfect information, and takes them into the decision trap, where the command leaders were in Sydney during the hostage event. Instead, we should judge whether their decisions were reasonable at the time, given what they knew.

Alternatively, if we evaluate our decision-makers based on whether their process was solid and whether their decision was reasonable at the time they made it, we encourage leaders to make decisions. Ideally, we want leaders to take decisions seriously. But also know that if they make reasonable choices, they will be protected, regardless of the outcomes.

Two caveats are appropriate here: First, overfocusing on decision process is also a trap. The goal is not perfect process; it is reasonable decisions made in time. Too much focus on process will lead to the process itself becoming the trap. Focus on making reasonable decisions.

Second, having a bias toward decision does not mean reckless decision-making or action. It means refusing to let uncertainty masquerade as prudence as a means of avoiding decisions.

Of course, to make reasonable decisions we must have good orientation.

HOW TO START: MAKING DECISIONS

Ask your direct reports: "Where do you need my approval but really shouldn't?" Then ask: "What decisions require my sign-off but never get a no?" Stop hoarding authority or wasting your time.

Orient or Die

Tactical units are obsessed with situational awareness or, more specifically, with orientation. This is because the key component for responding to a dynamic tactical event is the ability to understand what is taking place. In situations like Lindt Café, aligning what you think is happening with what is actually happening is the key to making effective decisions.

In elite teams the obsession with orientation is taken to another level. Massive investments are made into technologies that make improved orientation possible. Drones, robots, cameras, and listening devices are all employed to achieve orientation. But why?

All decisions are rooted in our ability to make sense of what is taking place. Without proper orientation we can, at best, make a blind guess as to what is occurring and how to solve it.

This is true at an individual level, and it is true at an organizational level. It is true in tactical situations, but it is also true in business. Yet this remains one of the most widely misunderstood topics in business literature and leadership courses.

If you spend any time around military or law enforcement training, you will inevitably encounter the work of Colonel John Boyd. Boyd's OODA loop may be the only concept more often cited in business books than the work of Sun Tzu.

OODA stands for Observe, Orient, Decide, Act, which Boyd identified as the critical components for making effective decisions. In popular literature you see this described as a circle where the faster you get through it, the better decisions you will make, and the more likely you are to outmaneuver your opponent.

The problem is that this interpretation is wrong. What's worse, it has led to a catastrophic misunderstanding about what Boyd meant and a generation of leaders who pay no attention to orientation, which inhibits their ability to gain situational awareness.

Mark McGrath put it bluntly: "The popular conception of OODA as a simple circular diagram is just plain wrong. In Boyd's actual 1995 sketch, in pencil on a yellow legal pad, orientation is the largest component and occupies the central position."

Orientation, then, is not one step among four. It is the primary step that matters most. In the words of Mark McGrath, "Orientation is a human's cognitive operating system. It shapes what we notice, value, believe, and think is possible. Observation, Decision, and Action are merely outputs of its current configuration. Orientation is not one box in a sequence. It is the nervous system of adaptation."

Your orientation is driven by your genetic heritage, cultural traditions, previous experiences, new information, and, most critically, your analytical and synthetic capabilities. This is the value of training and experience, and it is true in any type of decision you make and in any environment.

But your orientation can be both your greatest asset and your fatal weakness. Experience makes you better at sensing threats and opportunities, but it can also blind you to novel situations.

Kodak invented digital photography in the 1970s, but killed the project because their orientation, shaped by decades of success in film, could not process the utility of the technology or the threat it posed. They were oriented to their own comfort rather than to reality. And we know how that went for Kodak.

At Lindt, the command group's orientation never caught up to what operators on the ground could see.

It is essential that orientation is shared both up and down the chain of command. That is how teams continuously update their collective orientation.

You may recall when I discussed mission, I talked about the need to share the desired end state and commander's intent with the team. That is sharing orientation. The collaboration is how teams continuously update their collective orientation.

Achieving effective orientation must be a key part of the team culture and occur up and down the chain of command. Achieving and sharing orientation must be part of your culture.

One other thing that should be part of your culture is valuing diversity of perspective. By far the best argument for hiring people from diverse populations, diverse experiences, and diverse skills is that cognitive diversity provides much greater orientation.

As McGrath explains it, a team's orientation is the multitude of its perspectives. If your team members think differently, speak differently, act differently, and see the world differently, their orientation is unstoppable. If you ignore those perspectives or punish people for speaking from them, the advantage disappears.

If the organization is focused on always achieving effective orientation and sharing it, then decision-making becomes greatly simplified. The question then becomes who should make the decision?

HOW TO START: ORIENT OR DIE

Before your next major decision, stop and answer three questions: What do I think is happening right now? What information am I basing it on? Who has better situational awareness than I do on this issue?

Choosing the Chooser

A decision-making culture requires more than just telling people to decide. It requires putting decision authority in the right place. And in most organizations, that place is lower than leaders are comfortable with.

Kevin Cyr teaches that decision authority should flow to whoever possesses three qualities: (1) the training to understand the problem, (2) the situational awareness to see what is actually happening, and (3) the time to make the call before the window closes.

In many organizations, these three elements are scattered across different people. The person with the training sits in a command post. The person with situational awareness stands at the point of contact. And the person with authority to decide sits in an office somewhere checking boxes.

Elite teams solve this by pushing decision authority down to the person closest to the problem, who can see what is happening in real time, and has the expertise to make the call. This requires something that many organizations find deeply uncomfortable: trusting people at lower levels to make consequential decisions.

The mechanism that makes this work is commander's intent. Before any operation, the team leader clearly articulates what success looks like and why it matters. Not the specific actions to take, but the outcome to achieve and the constraints that bound acceptable methods. With that intent in mind, operators at every level can make decisions that serve the mission even when circumstances change faster than communication allows. The heuristic is not "here is what I want you to do" but "here is the result I want to see."

The Lindt Café siege failed precisely because decision authority was concentrated in commanders who lacked situational awareness, while operators with situational awareness lacked decision authority. The system was designed to prevent bad decisions by centralizing control, but it achieved the opposite. It prevented good decisions by disconnecting authority from information.

If your organization requires people to ask permission before acting, ask yourself this: Does the person granting permission have the training, situational awareness, and time to make a better decision than the person asking?

If the answer is no, you have built a system that will fail when it matters most. It is time to reorient how you make decisions.

> **HOW TO START:**
> **DELEGATING DECISION AUTHORITY**
>
> Pick a few recurring decisions. Identify who currently makes the decision. Now ask who has the best training, awareness, and time to make that decision? If those are different people, authority is in the wrong place.

70 Percent Is Close Enough

Any culture that requires absolute certainty before action will fall into the decision trap and fail under pressure. But the question is when do you have enough information to decide?

Commander Charles "Sid" Heal spent over three decades with the Los Angeles Sheriff's Department and served in four wars with the Marine Corps, beginning in Vietnam, as both an enlisted man and an officer, and became one of the most respected tactical thinkers in American law enforcement.

His wisdom, distilled from thousands of operations and countless hard lessons, cuts through the paralysis that afflicts decision-making under pressure.

He told me: "We don't have time to look for an optimal end state. We're only looking for a satisfactory one."

This principle, known in decision science as "satisficing," represents a fundamental shift in how leaders should think about choices under uncertainty. The search for optimal solutions is appropriate when you have unlimited time and complete information. But those are rare circumstances. In most cases, you have neither. Waiting for the perfect answer while acceptable answers pass you by is not prudence. It is abdication of responsibility.

Heal articulated a related truth that leaders must also internalize: "Doing the right thing at the wrong time is just as bad as doing the wrong thing at any time." Timing matters.

A good decision executed too late is functionally equivalent to a bad decision. The Lindt Café commanders may have believed they were making good decisions by waiting for more information, but the passage of time transformed every good option into a bad one.

An additional factor that should weigh into decision-making is whether the decision is reversible. Jeff Bezos likes to classify decisions into two categories: "Some decisions are consequential and irreversible or nearly irreversible, one-way doors, and these decisions must be made methodically, carefully, slowly, with great deliberation and consultation. If you walk through and don't like what you see on the other side, you can't get back to where you were before. We can call these Type 1 decisions."

But most decisions aren't like that. Bezos said, "They are changeable, reversible, two-way doors. If you've made a suboptimal Type 2 decision, you don't have to live with the consequences for that long. You can reopen the door and go back through. Type 2 decisions can and should be made quickly by high judgment individuals or small groups."

Bezos stresses the importance of treating these decisions differently and cautions to "never use a one-size-fits-all decision-making process." In his assessment "most decisions should probably be made with somewhere around 70 percent of the information you wish you had."

This 70 percent number is a popular approach advocated by everyone from Jeff Bezos to Kevin Cyr to General Stanley McChrystal.

Jeff Bezos also notes: "As organizations get larger, there seems to be a tendency to use the heavy-weight Type 1 decision-making process on most decisions, including many Type 2 decisions. The end result of this is slowness, unthoughtful risk aversion, failure to experiment sufficiently, and consequently diminished invention."

The best approach may be to use a combination of both of these criteria. Imagine a simple 2×2 grid: one axis is how much time you have; the other is how reversible the decision is. If the decision is reversible, time-constrained, or both, it makes sense to default to 70 percent information. Save the slow, heavy process for decisions that are both long-time horizon and irreversible one-way doors. For those limited decisions it makes sense to slow the process down, look for a higher level of certainty, and conduct a premortem.

HOW TO START: MAKING 70% DECISIONS

For your next significant decision, ask two questions: Is this reversible and what's the cost of delay? If you can undo it and delay costs more than being wrong, the 70 percent answer now beats the 90 percent answer next month.

90 Percent? It's Time for a Premortem

Many organizations conduct after-action reviews or postmortems for decisions that have gone poorly. After a project fails, after a mission goes wrong, after the damage is done, we gather to understand what happened. The problem is that this learning arrives too late to help the current situation.

The father of modern decision science, Gary Klein, has developed a technique that extracts those lessons before the failure occurs, which he calls a premortem. Here's how it works.

After a decision has been made but before it is executed, gather the team and ask them to imagine that the plan has failed spectacularly. Not that it might fail. That it has already failed. It's a fiasco. Then ask why.

Klein explains that when you ask people to critique a plan, they often encounter social pressure not to appear negative or disloyal. The premortem reverses this dynamic: by starting with the assumption that the plan failed, you give permission to identify weaknesses. You are not predicting failure. You are explaining an established fact. Research on prospective hindsight suggests premortems surface about 30 percent more potential failure modes than standard planning discussions.

Here is how to run a premortem in practice. After presenting your plan, tell the team: "Imagine it's six months from now. This project has failed completely. We're sitting here trying to figure out what went wrong. Take three minutes and write down all the reasons you can think of for why it failed."

Then go around the table, with each person sharing one reason. Keep cycling until you exhaust the list. What emerges will surprise you: Concerns that people have harbored privately suddenly appear in the open. Not every concern will prove valid, but you will know what your team is worried about and have the opportunity to address problems before they become failures.

If this sounds like a red team, that's because it is. It's a structured red team for high-consequence long-time horizon decisions and is extremely effective.

A culture that practices premortems and red teams is a culture that surfaces bad news before it becomes bad outcomes. It is a culture where dissent is not disloyalty but good counsel.

HOW TO START: RUNNING PREMORTEMS

After a big decision is made but before it's implemented, ask your team to "imagine this has failed spectacularly. Write down why." Go around the room. No rebuttals. Sort by likelihood and fix the preventable ones.

KEY PRINCIPLES

- Not deciding is deciding. Choosing not to act is choosing to surrender control to fate.
- Orientation is your cognitive operating system. It shapes what you notice, value, and think is possible.
- Push decision authority to whoever has the training, the situational awareness, and the time. That is almost never the person at the top of the org chart.
- 70 percent is close enough. Waiting for certainty costs more than imperfection.
- Premortems surface bad news before it becomes bad outcomes.

What Comes Next

Good decisions today do not guarantee good decisions tomorrow. The environment changes, competitors adapt, and what worked last year may fail next year. The decision machine requires continuous maintenance: ongoing training to keep pattern recognition sharp, regular debriefs to feed orientation, a relentless pursuit of improvement. Status quo is not neutral. It is decay.

The next chapter examines how elite teams build cultures of continuous improvement — where getting better is not a program but a way of life.

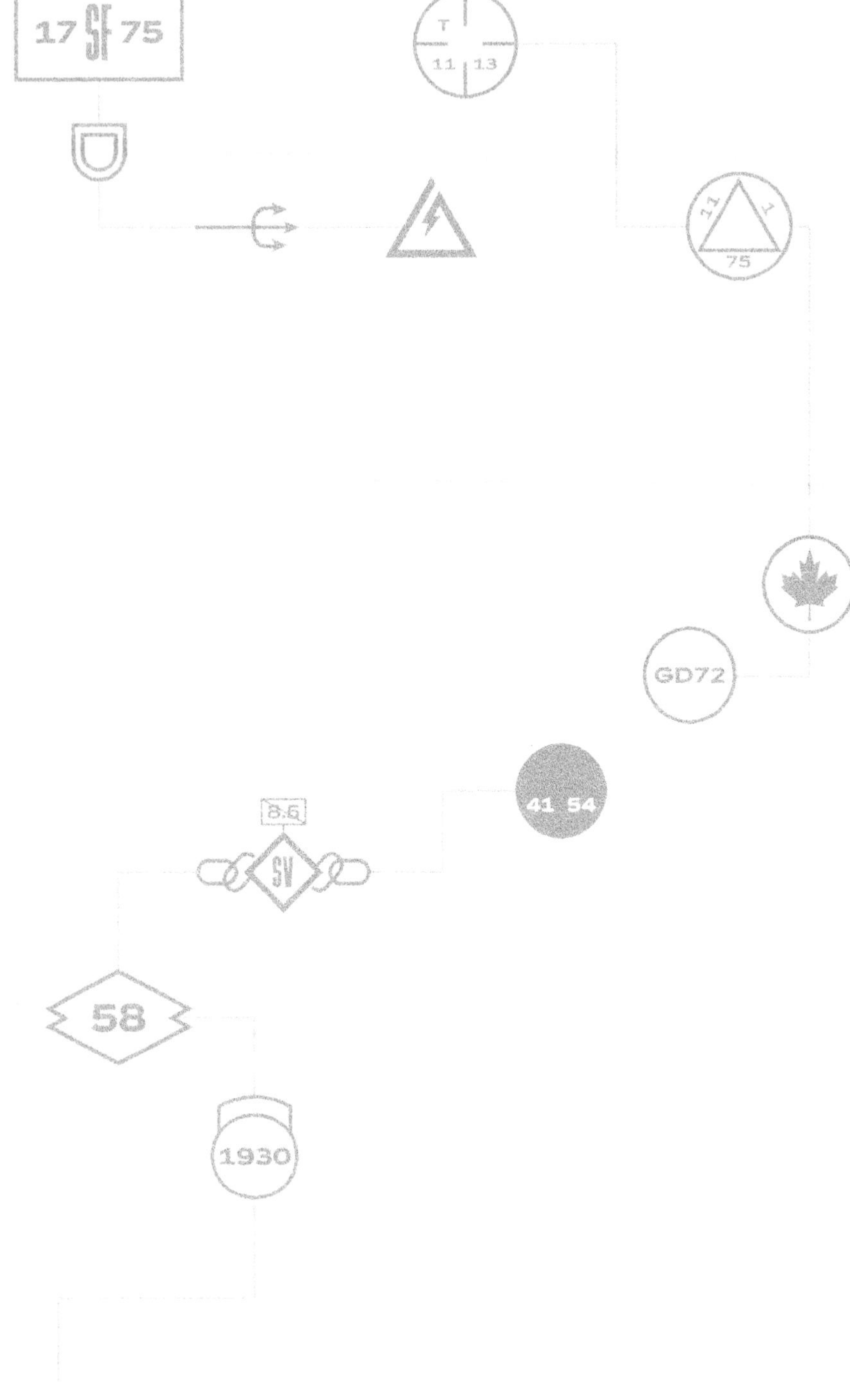

17 SF 75
T
11 13
11 1
75
GD72
41 54
8.6
SV
58
1930

CHAPTER EIGHT

IMPROVE CONTINUOUSLY

Embrace the Kaizen Lifestyle

I was watching one of the largest and most proficient SWAT teams in North America run night vision training: hostage rescue in the dark, stealth movement to contact with the hostage taker. They executed their movements flawlessly, cleared the structure, eliminated the threat. Perfect.

Then they gathered inside their training structure to debrief. For the next five minutes, they discussed the position of a hand on a doorknob and how a single door was opened.

One operator suggested that if the breacher had reached over this way rather than that way, the door would have opened more smoothly. They debated it.

They went back inside and ran it again. The next time, it was smoother. Five minutes of discussion, one small adjustment, a slightly better performance. And by the time the next element rotated through the training house, they had already been briefed on the change.

Their team commander, a friend, had asked me, when I arrived, to do a quick culture audit. Just a casual assessment: "Tell me what you see, and if anything negative catches your eye I want to know." After watching them train all day, he asked what I thought.

My response: "Your team was so quiet I could hear you breathing across the catwalk from me." Noise discipline is one of the most reliable indicators of how good a team is because it's hard to maintain. "The team had a five-minute constructive argument about how they wanted to open a doorknob, implemented it immediately, and had already briefed the next element before they rotated through. Your team is sorted, buddy. Only a really strong, healthy culture produces that good a process."

That team had long since moved past the big refinements. They weren't debating whether to go dynamic or deliberate, whether the stack was too tight or too loose. They had resolved those questions years ago. Now they were optimizing at the level of finger position on door hardware. And they would keep optimizing, because that's what elite organizations do. This chapter is about building that disposition into your organization.

Not continuous improvement as a program that you implement. Continuous improvement as a way of life.

The Japanese have a word for it: *kaizen*. Literally "good change." But the translation misses the essence. Kaizen isn't about change. It's about the relentless, daily, never-satisfied pursuit of getting a little bit better at something that matters.

This mindset needs to permeate both the organization's thinking and the individuals. From the top down, the organization must view kaizen as its lifestyle. From the bottom each individual must constantly think about how they can improve the team from their position.

To return to our operating system analogy, kaizen is about constantly upgrading the operating system. Elite teams never stop trying to improve. They treat every outcome as a teaching moment, embrace their failures, and look at success as something to build on, not as a destination.

Kaizen as a Lifestyle

Henry Ford revolutionized manufacturing with the assembly line. Before Ford, building a car was craft work. Skilled mechanics assembled entire vehicles, one at a time. Ford's insight was to break production into discrete steps, have each worker perform one task repeatedly, and pass the work down the line. It was revolutionary. Production times dropped from twelve hours per vehicle to ninety-three minutes. The Model T became affordable for ordinary Americans. Mass production changed the world.

But Ford's system had a critical flaw built into its design. When something went wrong on the line, the worker was expected to keep working. If you spotted a defect, you flagged it somehow, perhaps pulled it aside for an inspection later, but you didn't stop the line. Stopping the line was failure. Stopping the line meant everyone upstream got backlogged and everyone downstream sat idle. Stopping the line got you yelled at by your supervisor, or worse. As a result, only a supervisor could stop the line.

Toyota approached the problem quite differently. They implemented what they called the Andon cord system. Any worker on the production line could pull the cord and stop everything. Not just supervisors. Not just quality control inspectors. The newest employee on the floor had the authority to halt production.

Here's what made Toyota's approach fundamentally different from Ford's: When someone pulled the Andon cord, they weren't punished. Instead, the entire team gathered around to figure out why their teammate had to pull it. Because if you had to pull the cord, there's something wrong with the system. What are we doing wrong? Are we getting bad parts? Is the tooling wearing out? Is the process unclear?

Initially, everyone predicted disaster. The line would stop and start, stop and start. It was expected that production rates would plummet because you can't run a factory where anyone can shut everything down.

And initially, that's exactly what happened. Toyota's production rates were well below Ford's. The line stopped frequently as workers identified problems and teams gathered to solve them.

But very quickly, something remarkable happened. Toyota started outproducing all the Western manufacturers with better quality. They did this because every single person now had a vested interest in fixing the line. If I have to pull the cord, it means that you can't do your job. So, let's gather around and figure out the problem. Let's make this little change, then that little change, and eventually all those changes will add up. Problems that caused repeated stops quickly got solved permanently, and the Toyota system got better every day.

When researchers studied Toyota versus Western manufacturers, they found something counterintuitive. Toyota almost never had to stop the line anymore. Even though everybody could stop the line, Toyota had systematically eliminated the problems that would cause stops. As a result, the lines rarely came to a halt, and Toyota's production rates were the best in the world. All those individual people, all those little cogs in the wheel, made the system run better.

That is the heart of kaizen. It isn't a program you implement, it's a culture. Kaizen as a lifestyle says "we are going to get better every day, at something." By focusing the organization on constantly striving toward improvement, it permeates all levels and all roles in the organization.

Carol Dweck's research on mindset illuminates why this matters. Dweck distinguishes between fixed mindset and growth mindset.

People with a fixed mindset believe their abilities are static. They avoid challenges that might expose inadequacy, interpret effort as evidence of low ability, and see failure as a reflection of their fundamental worth.

People with a growth mindset believe abilities can be developed. They embrace challenges, view effort as the path to mastery, and treat failure as information about what to work on next.

Organizations have mindsets too.

A fixed-mindset organization protects its current way of doing things, interprets problems as threats, and punishes failure. Whereas, a growth-mindset organization welcomes problems as opportunities to improve, expects that current methods can always get better, and treats failure as learning. Toyota built a growth-mindset organization where they believed they could eliminate all problems if they worked at it hard enough. Ford, for all its early brilliance, built a fixed-mindset organization where certain problems were inevitable and there was no point in stopping the line to address them.

Kaizen is at the heart of all elite organizations. Having a passion and a system for improvement is a necessity to reach excellence. Elite teams send their operators all over the world to train with other organizations in a wide variety of disciplines.

Why would a team like Delta or SEAL Team Six send people to train with LAPD D-Platoon or LASD-SEB? Aren't Delta and ST6 the best trained operators in the world? Aren't they supposed to be the teams that others look up to? Sure, but only because they have a kaizen mindset. They collaborate with other units because other units have different experiences, training, and SOPs. They train with outside training companies because they might discover something that the tier 1 teams have not discovered. Simply put, they train with other people to find ways to improve their own systems and that is precisely why they are so good.

The business application of this is just as straight-forward. The organization must constantly be looking how it can improve itself and strive to make each of its people a source for organizational improvement.

Everyone has a unique perspective on the organization that can improve it.

The question isn't whether your organization needs continuous improvement. It does. The question is whether you've created the cultural conditions that encourage everyone to contribute to it.

> **HOW TO START: KAIZEN AS A LIFESTYLE**
>
> Identify one process in your organization that everyone knows is broken but nobody has fixed. Now ask why it hasn't been fixed. Is it because no one has permission to flag it? No mechanism to surface it? No expectation that anyone should? That broken process is a symptom. The real problem is whatever is preventing the person closest to it from pulling the Andon cord.

Leave the Team Better

The same is true from the individual level up. Everyone on the team must constantly ask themselves, how can I leave the team better than I found it?

One of my friends, John Montenegro, was the scout for LASD-SEB's Blue Team. The Scout is the most highly coveted, peer-leader position within the SEB team structure. Not unlike a senior non-commissioned officer (NCO) in a military unit, the Scout works alongside the Sergeant (aka Team Leader) in guiding all aspects of the team's performance. The Scout role is particularly critical to establishing and maintaining team culture. As the Blue Team Scout, Montenegro was living his dream. Mission planning, coordinating training, teaching, and running missions, he was living the life he planned. But as his retirement approached, he realized that his departure would negatively impact the unit unless he prepared the team in advance. So, with more than a year until his retirement, he stepped down as scout and turned the position over to the team member who would succeed him, Alex Lomeli.

Lomeli had been Montenegro's backup and was certainly ready for the challenge, but why would Montenegro give up the most coveted position on the team a year before he had to and become the lowest ranking guy on the team? Because, by leaving early, he was giving Alex Lomeli the opportunity to run the team with a safety net. He would still have Montenegro around as a consultant and a helper but would have a year to transition into the role. When I asked Montenegro what made him do it, his answer was simple: "I need to leave the team in a better place than I found it."

This idea of selfless humble stewardship rather than perceived ownership of a position is key. You don't own your role, your team, or your organization. You're merely taking care of it for the time you are there, and your obligation is to leave it and the organization in a better place than you received it.

Teammates who are trying to improve the organization make every large improvement possible.

With them, ordinary people accomplish extraordinary things because they're not wasting energy on self-protection and credit-seeking; they are working together for the common mission.

This desire to improve the team builds trust which enables the honest communication that makes elite teams. Selfless teammates think beyond their own careers. They make decisions that benefit people they'll never meet—successors who will inherit what they build.

The question is, does your team have the kind of people who will sacrifice themselves or their career for the good of the team or organization? Do they show up every day trying to be as professional as possible and working to improve themselves and the organization?

Done right these individual behaviors to improve the team interact directly with the organizational behaviors of Kaizen as a lifestyle and drive continuous improvement at all levels.

HOW TO START:
LEAVE THE TEAM BETTER

Write down the names of the two or three people on your team who could step into your role if you left tomorrow. If you can't name them, your departure would damage the organization — and that is a leadership failure, not a future problem. What are you doing this week to change that?

Status Quo Is Getting Fat

It is easy as a leader to believe that your organization can somehow reach a state of balance where it will continue to perform at its existing level without the need to develop. Sort of a state of equilibrium or status quo of excellence. But there is no status quo. Status quo is a comforting fiction. In any competitive environment, whether tactical operations, business markets, or professional sports, standing still means falling behind. If you are not improving, you are getting slowly worse.

Compounding that is the fact that your competitors are improving, your adversaries are adapting, and the environment is shifting. Accepting status quo in a changing competitive market is a decision to fail slowly. As a result it is essential that the team constantly resist the urge to stop moving forward and rest on successes of the past.

Think about it like fitness. You're either getting more fit, or you're getting more fat. There really isn't much in between. You don't maintain your fitness and weight. Every day you either move toward greater capability or toward atrophy. Skip workouts for a week, and you don't stay the same. You get weaker. The same principle applies to every skill, every capability, every competitive advantage your organization possesses.

If you are not trying to improve your shooting, your shooting is getting worse. If you are not trying to improve your fitness, your fitness is getting worse. If your organization gets caught up in a cycle of "we're okay, we're good, we're doing fine," you are not doing fine. You are gradually losing capability. Worse yet: If your organization gets sucked into the arrogance trap of "we are the best," it will likely be quite a while until you realize that you stopped being the best a long time ago.

Kodak had excellent processes for a film business that no longer existed. Blockbuster had excellent processes for a video rental business that no longer existed. Their orientations calcified while the world changed around them. As I discussed earlier, indecision is itself a decision with consequences.

The Hawthorne effect tells us that the moment your organization starts observing what you're doing, you will start making different choices. Maybe you don't eat the doughnut. Maybe you walk the stairs instead of taking the elevator. There's also a similar individual effect of simply paying attention. When you're measuring, when you're noticing, when you're actively engaged with your own improvement, you change behavior.

When you stop paying attention, when you assume things are fine, you drift. And drift only goes in one direction. Keep yourself, your team, and the organization focused on improvement and never fall into the trap of status quo.

> ## HOW TO START:
> ## IDENTIFYING SKILL DRIFT
>
> Identify the three capabilities most critical to your team's success. For each of them ask yourself, Is this better, the same, or worse than a year ago? Be honest. "The same" means worse, because your environment didn't stand still.

Measure What Matters Most

You can't improve what you don't measure. This is a management cliché because it's true. Without measurement, you're guessing. You think things are getting better, or you hope they're getting better, but you don't actually know.

The first thing they teach you in land navigation is to orient where you are. You can't plot a course to somewhere better if you don't know where you're starting from. Measurement is how you orient an organization. Remember from the last chapter that orientation is prime. Measurement of key metrics provides that orientation. So it is essential not only that we measure, but also that we measure the correct things to provide orientation that informs decisions.

What you measure is what people pay attention to. The factors the organization chooses to measure are the things team members regard as important. As a general rule, measure something, and it improves. Ignore something, and it drifts in a negative direction.

This connects directly to what I discussed earlier about status quo. If you're not getting on the scale, you're probably getting fat.

So it is essential that you not only measure key metrics but also that you choose carefully what you will measure, because frequently we measure really dumb things.

As discussed earlier, people do what's inspected, not what's expected. This is both a warning and an opportunity. It's a warning because if you inspect the wrong things, you'll get the wrong behavior. But it's an opportunity because if you inspect the right things, you'll drive improvement in the areas that actually matter.

Google learned this lesson building their engineering culture. They implemented blameless postmortems after every significant incident. The goal wasn't to find someone to punish. The goal was to understand what happened, why it happened, and how to prevent it from happening again. By measuring and inspecting the right things, learning rather than blame, they created a culture where engineers surfaced problems early rather than hiding them.

In other words, if it matters, measure it. And if you're measuring it, it better actually matter.

An organization can focus on only a limited number of items at once. As a result, there should be a limited number of metrics that the organization has its team focusing on simultaneously.

This is an area where a clear difference is visible between elite organizations and average organizations.

Elite organizations choose to measure what is directly tied to their performance and their process: Choosing to measure information that is actionable for the organization can result in change.

Less elite organizations tend to measure the easy stuff, regardless of their relevance to continuous improvement. Think back to the chapter on selection. Objective measures are easy because they are objective. That doesn't mean they are useful, and it is essential to resist the urge to just measure something because you can.

If you want to improve your organization, measurement is key.

HOW TO START: AUDIT YOUR METRICS

List every metric your team tracks. Circle the ones that directly connect to your mission and drive behavior. Any un-circled items are noise. Now find the most important outcome you don't measure and start measuring it this month.

Evolutions, Not Revolutions

When I interviewed James Kerr, one of his key insights about the All Blacks was their view that "the small things are the big things. The way you do one thing is the way you do everything." Elite organizations understand that excellence isn't found in grand gestures. It's found in the accumulation of lots of tiny actions done right. Small things, done consistently, compound into something extraordinary.

This is a profoundly different mindset than you typically see from less elite organizations. Most organizational improvement initiatives promise revolution. They throw everything out, start fresh, and try to transform completely. And most of them fail.

Not because the ideas are bad, but because revolution is inherently destabilizing. It loses institutional knowledge, creates resistance and overwhelms people's capacity to adapt.

Evolution works differently. Instead of trying to change everything at once, you improve one part. Then another. Then another. Each improvement is small enough to implement without drama, small enough that people can adapt, small enough that if it doesn't work you can reverse course without catastrophe. But small improvements compound. Each improvement creates a foundation for the next improvement. Over time, the cumulative effect exceeds what any single transformation could achieve.

Revolution is exciting. Evolution is effective. Trying to transform everything at once overwhelms organizations, breeds resistance, and usually fails catastrophically. Improving 1 percent per day doesn't just make you better. It makes you totally different over time.

That elite team debating hand position on a doorknob understood something that most organizations miss. They had long since solved the big problems. What remained was refinement at an increasingly granular level. And those refinements, accumulated over years, created performance that no amount of natural talent could match.

The organizations I've seen thrive over decades share this disposition. They treat kaizen as a lifestyle, not a program. They strive at an individual level to leave the team better than they found it. They measure what matters. And they pursue evolution rather than revolution.

Small changes equal big changes. Continuous improvement is what turns good into great. That's the secret hidden in plain sight across every elite organization that I've studied.

HOW TO START:
EVOLUTIONS, NOT REVOLUTIONS

Pick one thing your organization does every week that could be done one percent better. Not ten percent. Not transformed. One percent. Implement that improvement. Then do it again next week. The goal isn't the improvement itself — it's building the habit of looking for it.

KEY PRINCIPLES

- Status quo is loss. The organization that stops improving is already falling behind, whether it knows it yet or not.
- Kaizen is a lifestyle, not a program. Small improvements compound. One percent better every day creates something unrecognizable in a year.
- You don't own your role. You are a steward of it. Your obligation is to leave the team in a better place than you found it.
- Measure what matters. What you measure is what you optimize. If you aren't tracking it, you aren't improving it.
- Evolution beats revolution. Change everything at once and you get resistance, chaos, and failure. Change one thing at a time and you get compounding excellence.

What Comes Next

Continuous improvement requires a culture willing to push its limits. Small refinements compound, but only if the organization is willing to experiment, to try things that might not work, to push past the comfortable and familiar. An organization that only pursues safe improvements will only make safe improvements. The next chapter examines why the willingness to take calculated risks and embrace failure isn't a threat to elite performance. It is the precondition for it.

CHAPTER NINE

TAKE RISKS & EMBRACE FAILURE

It's Ok To Spin the Racecar

On January 29, 2013, a suspect kidnapped a five-year-old boy from a school bus and killed the bus driver. After the shooting in Alabama, the kidnapper took the child to an underground bunker that he had built on his property. The six-foot by eight-foot bunker was equipped with weapons, explosives, and a steel hatch door that was locked closed with a complex cable system that the suspect controlled from inside the bunker.

FBI activated the Hostage Rescue Team (HRT), who arrived on scene shortly thereafter.

Almost a week into the incident, after negotiations had failed and the behavioral scientists had determined that the hostage was in grave danger, HRT made the decision to tactically intervene.

HRT is the highest federal tactical asset in the United States. They are designed to resolve the most complicated problems. Viewed as the civilian law enforcement peer to the US military tier 1 units, HRT is well funded, exceptionally well trained, and certainly at the highest levels of the tactical profession. But even for HRT this was an incredibly complicated hostage rescue, that was exceptionally dangerous for the team members and for the hostage.

Yet there are times when calculated risks must be taken and preventing a child from being murdered is one of those times.

At the moment of truth, HRT operators breached the bunker door to retrieve the child. One of their team members jumped down into the hole only to discover that the suspect had booby trapped the opening with steel cables that left him entangled and hanging in the cables near the opening while the suspect emptied his gun trying to kill him.

Somehow, miraculously, he wasn't hit and was extracted from the hole while the breachers worked to clear the opening. Once the cables were cut, the same agent jumped down twelve feet into the hole and was able to grab and cover the child while one of his teammates, who also jumped down into the hole, neutralized the suspect.

There is little doubt what was in store for that child had HRT not intervened. He is alive and well because men who he had never met placed their lives on the line to save him.

This has always been one of my favorite things about the teams I work with. They are willing to take exceptional risks to save others. The selflessness and courage of these units is difficult to overstate.

The surprising thing about those risks is that they are never taken carelessly or recklessly. In the view of these units, risk is not something that is ever needlessly engaged.

My friend Kevin Cyr likes to say that "risk is the currency of a leader." Risk is not something to be avoided. In fact, avoiding risk is impossible. Rather risk is something to be carefully engaged to accomplish the goals of your organization.

Horror Movies and Porno Movies

There's a scene in the movie *Detroit Rock City* where a group of teenage boys are driving to a KISS concert and see an attractive girl hitchhiking on the side of the road. One of them wants to pull over and pick her up. Another one objects: "That's how horror movies start." A third chimes in: "Yeah, but it's also how porno movies start."

Same situation. Same risk. Two wildly different potential outcomes.

This is the reality of any enterprise where performance matters. Success and failure are not separated by vast chasms. They're separated by tiny margins, by decisions that could go either way, by risks that might pay off brilliantly or fail spectacularly. The team that wins the championship and the team that loses in the first round often have nearly identical talent. The startup that becomes a unicorn and the startup that flames out often started with nearly identical ideas.

If you want an organization that improves, you need an organization that takes risks. And if you want an organization that takes risks, you need to accept that some of those risks won't pay off. You can't have innovation without experimentation. You can't have experimentation without failure.

I drive race cars as a hobby. When I started, I spent several days at a track trying to improve my driving. I was struggling. I was going off the track, I was spinning the car. Then I had a morning where everything clicked. I didn't spin the car, didn't go off track, and felt like I really had it all figured out. At lunch I sat down with my coach Jeff Rodriguez to debrief the morning. When he asked me how everything went, I told him I felt great and that I think I finally figured it out.

He looked at the session's data and what he said forever changed the way I perceive risk: "Becker, the reason you feel like you're in control is because you're fucking slow! This is not supposed to feel like you are totally in control. Being fast is being on the edge of out of control. It should always be mildly scary. So, if you're totally comfortable, you're not getting better. You're just going slower."

I have learned in the years since that the same principle applies to organizations. If nobody is ever failing, nobody is pushing the edges. If every project succeeds, you're not attempting anything ambitious enough. You improve your shooting by missing, not by hitting. You improve your strength by lifting things you struggle with. If you spent the whole morning skiing and never fell down, you were not improving your skiing.

It is essential that organizations adopt a posture of pushing their limits and taking risks. This doesn't mean taking wild risks and it doesn't mean being stupid about it. But it does mean that you need to fail at some of your experiments and that you need to push the limits of what your organization is capable of.

At an individual, team, and organizational level, getting better means pushing past your current limits. This means spinning the race car from time to time. Strive to create an environment where experimentation is encouraged and failure is embraced as a learning tool.

> ## HOW TO START:
> ## TEST YOUR RISK APPETITE
>
> Name your team's last three big risks taken. If you can't find three, you're focused on safety at the expense of growth. Now ask: What happened to the people whose risks didn't pay off?

Embrace Failure

Along with a willingness to take risks, a healthy culture must also have a healthy appetite for failure. The horror movie is always the most likely result. As an organization you have a culture of embracing failure as a teaching tool.

Dr. Dan Dworkis is the Chief Medical Officer for the Mission Critical Team Institute and an emergency room physician in Los Angeles. Dan and his team are often the only thing that stands between a severely injured patient and death.

Like any busy ER Physician death is always present in Dworkis' world and sometimes no matter what he and his team do, they are destined to fail and death wins.

When I interviewed Dworkis on The Debrief, I asked him how he handles the death of patient expecting him to talk about proactive therapy or

PTSD. What he said surprised me and gave me a new perspective on engaging with failure.

When a patient dies, Dworkis gathers the team at the bedside, places a hand on the deceased, and says to the patient: "Thank you for teaching me. I am sorry that all I could do for you today was learn . . . I am sorry all I could today was learn"

When Dworkis said this, I felt the air leave the room. I could see the pain in his face as he recalled who knows how many patients, they were unable to save. This is a powerful ritual, and it would certainly be easier to just walk away and try never to think about that patient again.

But rather than blocking failure out and moving on, Dworkis chooses to look failure square in the eye and immediately trigger the learning process.

This is the mindset of an elite team and the kind of growth mindset that all organizations need.

Jennifer Prohaska is a clinical psychologist who works on more than thirty officer-involved shootings a year and consults with more than fifty public safety agencies. She has learned something in working on critical incidents that every leader needs to hear: The difference between those who bounce back from failure and those who don't has almost nothing to do with how severe the failure was. It's all about how they view it.

Dr. Prohaska's approach to healthy coping centers on what she calls the three Rs: Recognize, Respect, and Return.

- **Recognize** that something happened and it registered with you emotionally. When your startup runs out of runway or a cofounder betrays your trust or an operation goes sideways, you acknowledge the reality.
- **Respect** what you're feeling. Pause and give that emotion its moment, but just a moment.
- **Return** to what you need to do next. Process it, learn from it, then move forward.

Don't punish failure and don't run away from it. Engage with it and learn every possible lesson it has to teach.

This means not trying to find someone to blame or seeing yourself or your organization as a victim every time something goes wrong. Rather place your hand on the patient and make sure that you learn what each failure offers to teach you.

The road to success is always paved by failures.

Dr. Prohaska has largely abandoned the term *resilience* in favor of *antifragility*, a term first coined by Nassim Taleb in his book *Antifragile*. The distinction matters. Resilience is bouncing back to your original form after being knocked off equilibrium. Antifragility is using negative experiences to become better by asking how do I use this to make me a better human? Whatever challenges our organizations endured, how do those losses make us better?

This isn't unrealistic positivity. It's recognizing that the course of your river has changed, and your final destination can be better if you're intentional about it.

Dr. Prohaska calls this the five-year test: Five years from now, how do you want this failure to look? Do you want to be the bitter founder still complaining about what went wrong, or someone who used that experience to build something even better?

> ## HOW TO START: EMBRACING FAILURE
>
> Describe your team's most recent failure. What happened to the person responsible? Were they supported and developed, or marginalized? That is your actual failure culture regardless of what leadership says.

Process v. Outcome

It is also important that you understand the difference between your process and the outcome that results. In tactical operations, a team can only control their training, fitness, preparation, and decision-making. They can't control what the suspect does or a thousand other variables. As a result, there are many potential outcomes where no matter what the team does it won't end well.

Think back to the Lindt Café. NSW's TOU was highly trained, they were prepared and their plan likely would have saved lives. But they did not have control over when they launched and therefore were not in control of what resulted.

The same is true with organizations. Although you can control your own processes, you cannot necessarily control the outcomes of those decisions. You do not control a lot of variables. So the best approach seems to be the organization must focus on improving processes and on when debriefing failures focus on how processes could have been improved to get a different result.

When organizations focus on their process, ensuring it aligns with their values and expertise, they can handle outcomes they didn't plan for. The same applies in business. You can control your product quality, team culture, and strategic decisions. You cannot control the economy, competitor actions, or regulatory changes.

"If your process is solid and you've backed it in line with your values," Dr. Prohaska explains, "the outcome becomes more capable of handling."

That's why some founders can lose everything and start again with optimism, while others become permanently embittered. It's not about the magnitude of the loss. It's about where they located their sense of control.

Dr. Prohaska offers a simple lesson: "Don't feed the weeds."

You have weeds in your mental garden: the things you can't control, the injustices you've suffered.

You also have plants: the things you can control, the actions you can take, the growth you can pursue.

Where you focus your mental energy determines what grows. After a business failure, you can focus on how the market was unfair or how investors didn't understand your vision. Those might be true, but they're weeds. Or you can focus on what you learned and what you'll do differently next time. Those are plants. Both narratives might be accurate. Only one is useful.

Gary Klein offers a diagnostic query to assess whether someone has learned from experience: Ask them about their last failure. If they can't recall one, or they blame external factors, or they describe it as something that happened to them rather than something they participated in, they haven't been learning. Ten years of experience can be one year repeated ten times if you're not extracting lessons from what goes wrong.

The organizational challenge is creating conditions where failure becomes learning rather than punishment. Organizations that punish failure get employees who hide mistakes, avoid risks, and never attempt anything ambitious enough to fail at. Organizations that treat failure as information get employees who experiment, learn rapidly, and compound their improvements over time.

As she put it: "Bad incidents make strong people." But only if you frame them correctly. Only if you recognize, respect, and return. Only if you focus on process rather than outcome. Only if you refuse to feed the weeds.

> **HOW TO START: PROCESS V. OUTCOME**
>
> Look at the last few failures your organization has had. After the event did you spend time figuring out where your process had gone awry and how to fix it? Or did you figure out who to blame for the result and feed the weeds?

The Debrief Closes the Loop

There is a reason my podcast is called *The Debrief*. After-action reviews or debriefs are a critical part of tactical culture. Debriefs are how elite teams extract learning from experience and continuously improve their decision-making.

The goal of any tactical debrief is to uncover truth. What actually happened? What did we miss? How do we get better? What the team chooses to measure in debriefs can vary widely by how skilled the team is.

In elite organizations the focus is on the process and on the orientation. We expected X and got Y, what caused that difference? We perceived A happened, but B happened; what information was available that would have shown us this, and how could we have gotten it? We actually did X and we wanted to do Y, how come? Why did that happen?

The goal of elite team debriefs is measuring the accuracy of their orientation to reality. Then trying to improve everything that did not go as expected. In the process they are intentionally harvesting the lessons that risk and failure have to offer.

Think about the team we discussed who asked themselves how they could have opened the door a little more effectively. This is an elite growth mindset. Every operation is a chance to get better. Every failure is a chance to learn. Everything we measure matters to our operations.

By contrast, in more average organizations, the question in a debrief is usually more focused on errors than growth. Who made a mistake and why? No mistakes, debrief done! But no debrief means no improvement.

A critical factor at play here is that adopting a growth mindset that encourages looking at failure. The team that grows from every debrief looks forward to the debrief. The team that views debrief as punishment dreads it and finds a way not to do it.

One of the most common differences I see in the critical incidents covered by my guests on *The Debrief* is that the elite organizations will have always had internal debriefs by the time I talk to them, no matter how poorly the event went. The less elite teams almost never have, even if it went well.

In the corporate world, most debriefs are done wrong. They focus narrowly on the actions people took. What did you do? What was the sequence of events? What could you have done differently? Often this is simply in an effort to find blame rather than learn from failures.

Gary Klein points out that these questions miss the point entirely. "Too many debriefs are just narrowly focused on the actions people took and not on how they were sizing up the situation."

The real expertise—the pattern recognition that enables rapid response—lives in how people were making sense of what they observed. When we focus only on actions, we catalog behaviors without transferring the cognitive patterns that enabled those behaviors. We learn what happened without understanding why it happened that way.

Klein developed what he calls the cognitive debrief methodology. Instead of asking what did you do? you ask, what were you seeing or hearing? What were you *not* seeing or hearing that you expected to? Is there anything that got you suspicious because it wasn't happening? These questions explore the sense-making process and orientation that underlies decisions.

When I first heard Klein explain this distinction, I responded: "That's where the magic is." And it is. The magic is not in the actions themselves but in the cognitive framework that generated those actions. Transfer the framework, and you transfer the capability.

The debrief feeds orientation. What McGrath called the need to continuously reorient, what Boyd described as updating your correspondence to reality, happens through the debrief process. You take the feedback from actions, examine it through the cognitive debrief methodology, and use what you learn to refine your mental models.

By figuring out what went right and what went wrong and, more importantly, why you made the decisions you did, you are changing the way you will perform on the next project. More importantly you are sharing that knowledge through the entire team which means the entire team is getting better.

Studies of teams across domains show performance gains of roughly 20 to 25 percent when they use structured debriefs. That is not a marginal gain. That is the difference between good and elite. And the investment required, averaging around eighteen minutes per debrief, is trivial compared to the return.

Three simple changes can transform most organizations' debriefs:

- First, add cognitive questions: What were you noticing? What were you worried about? What did you expect to happen next?
- Second, focus on the transitions: When did the situation change? What cues told you? Who saw them first?
- Third, capture the learning formally: What will we notice sooner next time?

The goal is not to assign blame but to understand systems. Klein warned that when debriefs become official documents, they get sanitized. The real failures—the moments where someone failed to anticipate or recognize—never get included because no one wants to damage careers. He said, "The institutional mechanism for preserving lessons actually destroys them."

If people suspect that honest debriefs will be used to damage careers, they will feed the system sanitized stories instead of truth.

I have seen this for years. It is not unusual that the original candid debrief I hear from a team transforms into a hero story as it moves up the organization and risk of consequence increases. It often goes from self-reflective and critical to a sanitized story that no longer represents what happened and worse serves no one.

In fact, the first question I ask people after an event is always "what went wrong?" If their answer is nothing, we are likely done discussing the case. We usually learn from mistakes and if you are not self-critical that process quickly becomes a waste of time.

Elite teams embrace failure by building cultures where candor is not just permitted but expected; where the question what did you miss? is asked with curiosity rather than accusation; and where the answer "I didn't see it coming" is the beginning of a learning conversation rather than the end of a career.

That is what the debrief is for. It is not for punishment or documentation. Its purpose is reorientation and improvement on future work.

HOW TO START:
DEBRIEF GROUND RULES

Draft three to five ground rules for your debriefs. For example: Critique the process, not the person. Focus on thinking, not just actions. Post them visibly and read them at the start of every session.

KEY PRINCIPLES

- Risk is the currency of a leader. The question is never whether to spend it, but how wisely to spend it.
- If nobody is ever failing, nobody is pushing the edges. Comfort is a sign you have stopped improving.
- Organizations that punish failure get employees who hide mistakes. Organizations that treat failure as information get employees who compound their growth.
- Focus on process, not outcome. You control your preparation and your decisions. You cannot control everything that follows.
- The debrief closes the loop. Performance gains come not from what happened but from understanding why it happened that way.
- Recognize. Respect. Return. Failure is a teacher, not a verdict.

What Comes Next

Nine practices. One operating system. Culture does not emerge from any single chapter but from the cumulative effect of all nine working together. The practices reinforce each other: you cannot enforce standards without servant leaders, cannot collaborate without strong people willing to challenge the mission, cannot improve continuously without the courage to take risks and learn from failure. The Conclusion examines how to put the full system into motion.

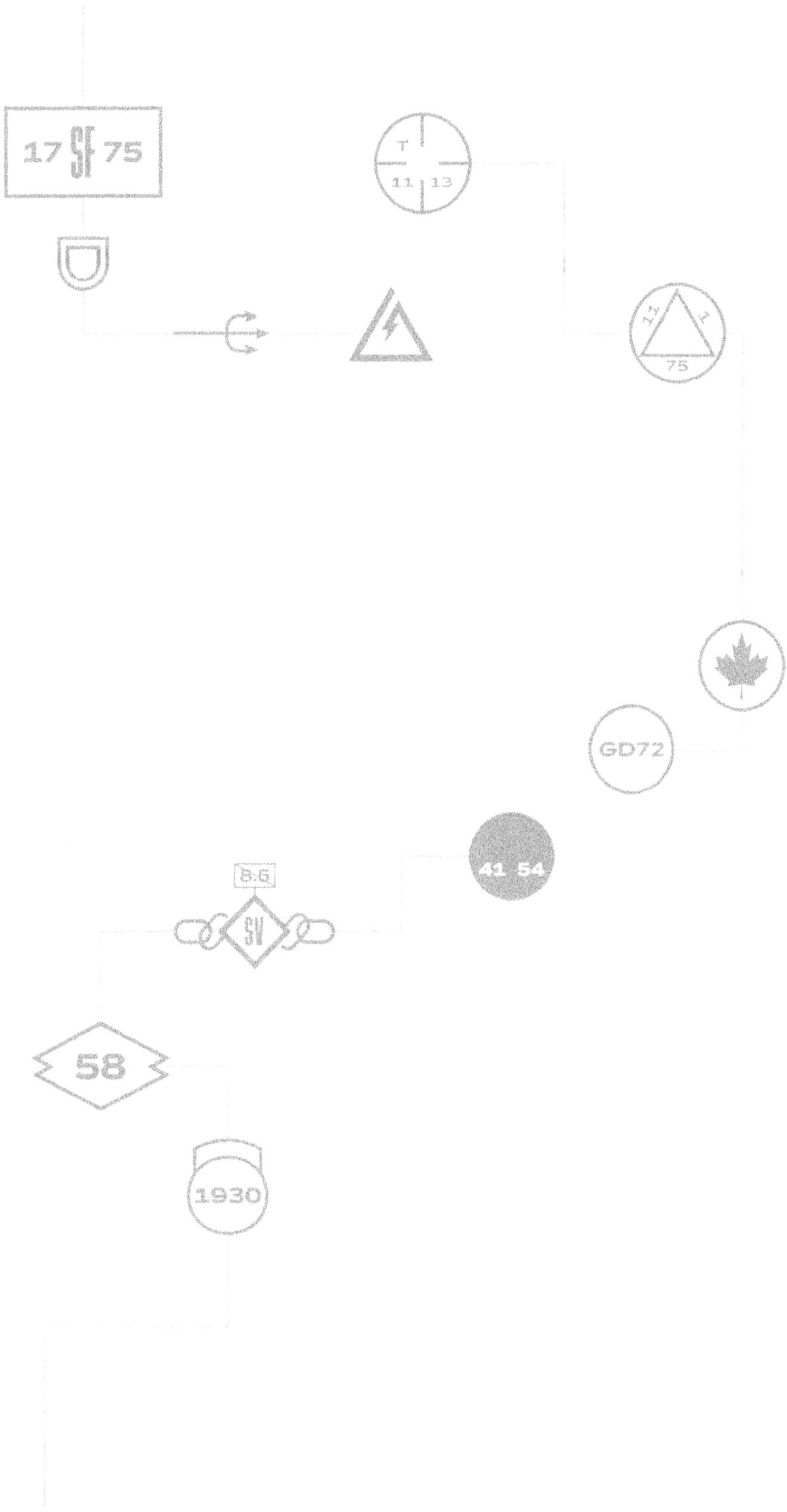
17 SF 75
T
11
13
11
1
75
GD72
41 54
8.6
SV
58
1930

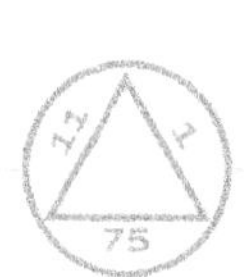

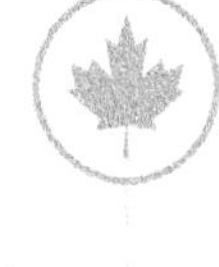

PUTTING IT ALL TOGETHER

What Comes Next

Early in my career, I was assisting a man named Sid Heal with a class on diversionary devices. I mentioned him earlier. Sid was a Marine Corps Chief Warrant Officer-5, four-time combat veteran, and Commander of the Los Angeles County Sheriff's Special Enforcement Bureau. He would become my mentor, my friend, and the single greatest influence on my professional life.

After the class, a guy asked if he could copy Sid's slides and outline. This was Sid's intellectual property—curricula he'd spent years developing.

Sid handed it over and said, "Yeah, there you go."

I was stunned. "Why would you give that away?"

Sid looked at me like I'd missed the most obvious point in the world. "You never hoard information. Information is safety. If this guy teaches somebody else, and that person doesn't get killed because of something they learned, then my work made a difference in a way I'll never even know."

The ability to help confers the responsibility to help. I've spent my entire adult life learning what makes elite teams elite. I don't want that knowledge to disappear when I do.

The principles in this book aren't secret. What separates elite organizations is that they really do what others only talk about. They build cultures intentionally when others let culture happen by accident.

As we said at the beginning of this journey, your organization runs on an operating system that you may not have chosen.

Nine chapters later, you understand what that operating system looks like when it's built intentionally.

You know why the default is toxic and why intentional culture beats accidental culture every time. You understand why effective leaders must be built and have seen how rigorous selection helps you pick humble and strong people that challenge you in ways that make the organization better. You have also seen how your standards are defined by what you tolerate, not what you proclaim. You've learned that deliberate collaboration harvests collective wisdom, that decision authority belongs wherever the best information resides, and that organizations either improve continuously or decline by default. You've also learned that risk and failure are where improvement and greatness are born.

The nine practices all work as a system. Implement them together and they compound. Leave one out and the others become harder to sustain. That's the mechanics of elite performance, no matter who you are or what team you are on or leading.

The nine practices I have introduced to you are simple to understand. Simple does not mean easy. The hard part is doing them day after day, when it's inconvenient, when it's uncomfortable, when it would be easier to let standards slide or avoid the difficult conversation.

Every choice either reinforces the culture you want or undermines it. There is no neutral ground.

The tactical units I've worked with don't have the luxury of getting culture wrong. When they fail, people die. Your stakes may be different, but they're higher than you think. Organizations that should thrive, instead, stagnate. Careers derail. Talented people leave because the culture doesn't deserve them. The costs of bad culture accumulate invisibly until the damage is done. Leaders who understand this build teams that transcend any individual member.

Look back at the nine practices. Central to all of them is putting something ahead of yourself.

Building culture intentionally requires humility about what you don't know. **Servant leaders** eat last, own the losses, and share the wins. **Rigorous selection** means protecting the culture over acquiring talented individuals who might threaten it. **Building strong people** means tolerating the discomfort of being challenged. **High standards** mean having conversations you'd rather avoid. **Deliberate collaboration** means admitting that the warehouse guy might catch what ten executives missed. **Effective decision-making** means pushing authority to others. And **continuous improvement** means accepting that you're never finished. **Risk and Failure** mean putting your ego and maybe your career on the table in an effort to build a better organization.

The practices only work when team members and leaders internalize a simple truth: It's not about you. It's about your people and your mission.

Build a Cathedral

Peter Drucker, in *The Practice of Management*, tells the story of three stonecutters who were each asked the same question: "What are you doing?"

The first replied, "I am making a living."

The second kept hammering while he said, "I am doing the best job of stonecutting in the entire county."

But the third stonecutter looked up with a visionary gleam in his eyes and said, "I am building a cathedral."

All three were doing the same work. But their perspectives differed entirely. The third stonecutter understood that his labor was part of something far greater than himself, and it was a vision that would outlast his own lifetime. Purpose transforms labor into legacy.

Cathedral thinking is undertaking work that has purpose and requires a long time to complete, laboring in the present in the service of future generations. Building something beyond yourself.

Elite tactical units today are operating on decisions that were made by leaders decades ago. The culture, the training protocols, the selection criteria, the operational doctrine were all created by people who knew they would not be there to see the full fruits of their labor.

John Kolman, who founded the National Tactical Officers Association. Sid Heal, who wrote more than 160 articles and books on tactical operations. These tactical pioneers built institutions, not just teams. They shared freely so that units they would never meet would benefit from their hard-won knowledge. They built structures that still exist long after they have left their positions.

This is the ultimate expression of selfless leadership. When you serve the next generation, you're not just passing on knowledge, you're passing on capability.

Servant leaders think this way about their organizations. They are not building for themselves. They are building for the people who will come after them, for the missions that have not yet been conceived, for the challenges that do not yet exist. Their ego is subordinated to their legacy. And that is perhaps what Brian Driscoll was thinking about when he refused the directive to supply names of his fellow FBI agents.

Put differently, great leaders plant trees under which they will never sit simply because they know that others will benefit. We must always be thinking about how we can benefit the organization and its future members beyond our tenure.

What cathedral are you building? Who will it serve and who will complete it after you are gone?

Finding My Purpose

As I said at the beginning, I started my business when I was seventeen years old. While I would love for you to believe that I had a grand plan at that age and am a blend of Marvel's Tony Stark and a boy genius, it's simply not the case. I was fortunate to end up in amazing places, surrounded by geniuses who took pity on me and let me absorb information in their shadow. That's the real story. Just a lot of luck, insatiable curiosity, and the good sense to never turn down free training.

But here's what that story leaves out: why I started.

Money. Pure and simple. I wanted to be rich. I saw an unmet need in the rock-climbing market, and I had enough hustle to fill it, so I thought: I will be rich. The initial impulse was entirely self-interest.

For years, that sustained me. The business grew. Every milestone confirmed my thesis that if I worked hard and filled a need, I would find success.

I don't know exactly when the transition happened and I can't point to a single moment when I stopped thinking about selling things and started thinking about protecting people.

But I do know when I first noticed it: Louis Pompei's funeral.

That was the moment I recognized the shift. Not when it happened, but when I finally saw it clearly. The mission had become protecting people. Not as a marketing message, but as an actual purpose that shaped every decision.

Now, nearly forty years later, that fire still burns bright. Maybe brighter than ever. Purpose never gets old. Every time I hear that someone was saved by our gear, that purpose renews itself.

Final Thoughts

Remember Milena, the young purchasing clerk who shredded an ISO consultant and eventually became a director? Here is the rest of that story.

Several months after we implemented our ISO program, I asked her to create a new form to ferret out where we were having problems between two departments. She disagreed and wanted to discuss it. I told her I was getting in my car to drive to a meeting and would call her on the way.

She argued with me for an hour on the way to my meeting. She argued with me for almost an hour on the way back. When I told her I was five minutes away and would see her when I got there, she hung up.

Her boss asked her who she had been arguing with all day. "Jon," she said.

"So you've been arguing with the founder of our company for two hours? The CEO? The boss of your boss's boss?"

She approached me when I arrived, apologetic and apparently concerned. "I am sorry I argued so long. This is your company and I'll do whatever you want me to do. But I have to ask, did I just cost myself a job?"

"No. Absolutely not. There is more going on here than you are seeing, so let's just implement it and reassess in a couple months."

We implemented the form. Ninety days later, she walked into my office with the first report. "You were right. I was wrong." Then she asked: "Why the hell did you let me argue with you for two hours?"

"Because if I kill your passion, I will never reignite it."

She was wrong about the form. But I hadn't protected her argument, I had protected her will to argue. That willingness is rare and precious. People who will speak truth to power are valuable. And once you destroy their will, you don't get it back.

I am truly fortunate to be surrounded by amazing people who make me better every day. I am profoundly grateful for them. They push me to heights I did not know I could achieve and prevent me from ever taking the easy path.

The process of creating this book has been a true test of that system and of how much I believe in these principles.

My goal when I set out was to write the best possible leadership book that captured all of the amazing lessons I have learned from the teams I work with. But, doing so is not for the faint of heart or weak of motivation.

This book has been read and reread by so many of my friends that I am kind of surprised anyone is still taking my calls.

The process for me has been much like I imagine the sharpening process feels for a knife. Repeatedly getting dragged violently across a stone with the hope that the pain you are enduring is making you sharper.

There were so many times that I THOUGHT this book was done only to have someone raise a significant issue that required a significant rewrite or restructure.

Every time I found myself asking myself isn't it "good enough?" And every time I was fortunate enough to be surrounded by strong people who would remind me that there is no "good enough" because what you tolerate is your new standard.

Elite teams are elite because they go above and beyond what "normal" teams are willing to do. They build an intentional culture of excellence that constantly drives them toward greatness.

YOU NOW HAVE ALL THE TOOLS I AM AWARE OF TO MAKE THAT HAPPEN. I HOPE THAT YOU USE THEM TO MAKE A REAL DIFFERENCE IN YOUR WORLD.

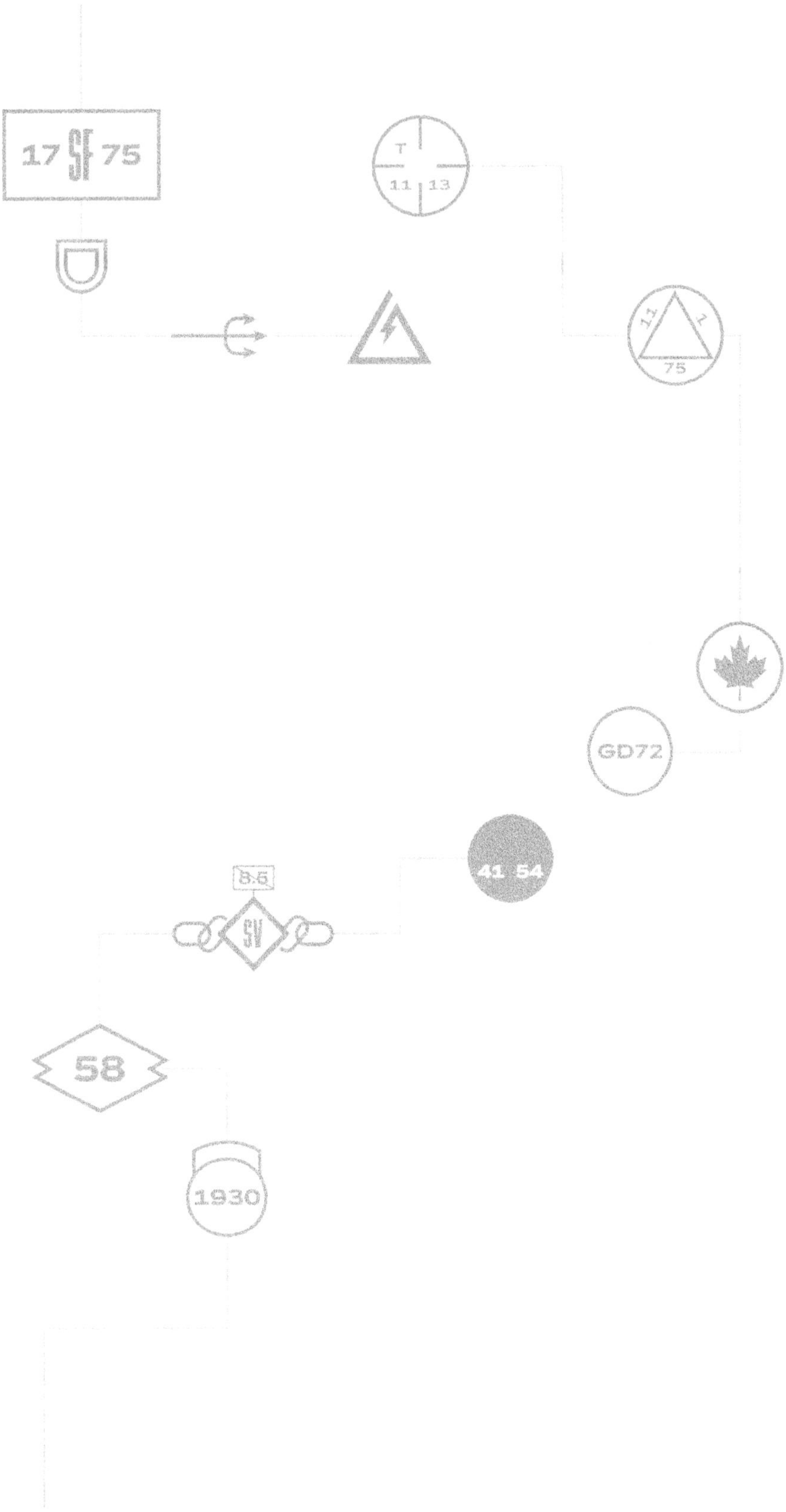
17 SF 75
T
11 13
11 7
75
GD72
41 54
8.5
SV
58
1930

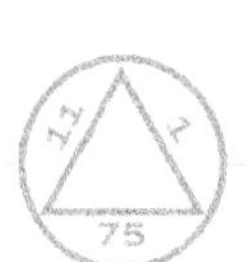

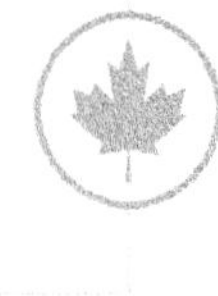

NOTES

These notes are provided to support further exploration of concepts not as exhaustive citations of concepts. They are also provided to avoid burdening the narrative with extensive context.

Introduction

The account of the Battle of FOB Ghazni is compiled from multiple sources: the official Medal of Honor citation from the Congressional Medal of Honor Society; US Army official records; and the author's interview with Master Sergeant Earl Plumlee on The Debrief podcast. Plumlee received the Medal of Honor from President Joe Biden on December 16, 2021. Staff Sergeant Michael H. Ollis of 10th Mountain Division received the Distinguished Service Cross posthumously for shielding Polish Army Lieutenant Karol Cierpica from a suicide bomber. The attack occurred on August 28, 2013, at Forward Operating Base Ghazni, Ghazni Province, Afghanistan. Plumlee served with C Company, 4th Battalion, 1st Special Forces Group (Airborne).

The estimate of training with thousands of tactical teams is based on the author's business records spanning 1986 to 2024, including formal training contracts, equipment demonstrations, and consulting engagements with federal, state, local, and international tactical units.

The operating system metaphor for organizational culture has been developed by multiple organizational theorists. For a comprehensive treatment, see Daniel Coyle, The Culture Code: The Secrets of Highly Successful Groups.

What you tolerate is your standard emerged as a recurring theme across author interviews with tactical commanders. The concept reflects the gap between stated values and actual organizational behavior.

Lou Gerstner's transformation of IBM is documented in Louis V. Gerstner Jr., Who Says Elephants Can't Dance? His observation about culture's power to resist change provides a corporate parallel to tactical leadership challenges.

Commander Charles "Sid" Heal's tactical decision-making philosophy is from author interview, The Debrief podcast, episode 1, 2024. Heal served over three decades with the Los Angeles Sheriff's Department.

Chapter 1: Build Culture Intentionally

Bataclan Theatre rescue account compiled from author's direct interview with a Brigade de Recherche et d'Intervention team leader who participated in the November 13, 2015, operation. The incident, which killed 130 people across multiple Paris sites including 90 at the Bataclan Theatre, is extensively documented in French government reports and international media, including the French parliamentary commission report on the November 13, 2015, attacks (2016). Additional context from Daniel Psenny and Jean-Pierre Filiu, "Inside the Bataclan: The Full Story," Le Monde, November 2016.

Simon Sinek's framework is presented in Simon Sinek, *Start With Why: How Great Leaders Inspire Everyone to Take*

Action. Author interview with organizational culture research, 2024.

Johnson & Johnson's Credo, authored by Robert Wood Johnson in the 1940s, states, "We believe our first responsibility is to the patients, doctors and nurses." James Burke credited the Credo as decisive during the 1982 Tylenol crisis response. See "Tylenol and the Legacy of J&J's James Burke," Knowledge at Wharton, Wharton School of the University of Pennsylvania.

Van France joined The Walt Disney Company in March 1955 and established Disneyland's cast training program (the "University of Disneyland"), which later evolved into Disney University. The "backstage/onstage" philosophy is attributed to France in Doug Lipp, Disney U: How Disney University Develops the World's Most Engaged, Loyal, and Customer-Centric Employees (McGraw-Hill Education, 2013).

The Nordstrom employee handbook story, while widely recounted in business literature, reflects the company's actual cultural philosophy. See Robert Spector and Patrick D. McCarthy, The Nordstrom Way: The Inside Story of America's #1 Customer Service Company (Wiley, 1995).

Chapter 2: Build a Team of Selfless Leaders

It's not about you captures the fundamental mindset shift required for elite team membership. The phrase emerged from the author's observations across multiple tactical unit selection programs over three decades.

"Leaders eat last" philosophy is documented in Simon Sinek, Leaders Eat Last: Why Some Teams Pull Together and Others Don't. See also Marine Corps leadership traditions discussed in Thomas E. Ricks, Making the Corps (Scribner, 2007).

Research on humble leadership is compiled in Edgar H. Schein and Peter A. Schein, Humble Leadership: The Power of Relationships, Openness, and Trust.

Jordan MacWilliams, interview by Jon Becker, "Critical Incident Review: Jordan MacWilliams Charged with Murder for Shooting a Hostage Taker," The Debrief with Jon Becker, Episode 21, 2024.

The FBI leadership crisis under Acting Director Brian Driscoll illustrates the consequences of culture failure. Driscoll's actions, including his "I am one of those employees" statement to FBI staff, are documented in Ken Dilanian et al., "FBI's Acting Director Tells Agents Not to Defy Orders," NBC News, February 1–2, 2025; "Driscoll Fired from FBI," CNN, August 7, 2025; Emil Bove memo on FBI leadership transition, CBS News, February 1, 2025.

The Marine Corps tradition of officers eating last represents cultural practice rather than formal doctrine, embodying the Corps' leadership philosophy of putting troops first. See Ricks, Making the Corps. The practice is discussed in Sinek, Leaders Eat Last, pp. 1–7.

Kevin Cyr's leadership development insights are from author interview, The Debrief podcast, 2024. Cyr served as Emergency Response Team Commander with the Royal Canadian Mounted Police.

Steve Jobs's uncompromising standards at Apple are documented in Walter Isaacson, Steve Jobs. Jobs's famous "A players hire A players, B players hire C players" philosophy appears throughout Isaacson's account of Apple's culture.

The concept of extreme ownership and its relationship to standards is documented in Jocko Willink and Leif Babin, Extreme Ownership: How US Navy SEALs Lead and Win.

Mike Hillmann's insights on LAPD SWAT standards and culture are from author interview, The Debrief podcast, 2024.

Hillmann served as LAPD SWAT team leader during critical periods in the unit's history.

Lee McMillion's perspective on maintaining standards in elite units is from author interview, The Debrief podcast, 2024. McMillion served in LAPD's D-Platoon (SWAT) and provides insights on the unit's culture of excellence.

The quote, "People will forget what you said, people will forget what you did, but people will never forget how you made them feel," is widely attributed to Maya Angelou, though the exact origin does not appear in her published works. The sentiment captures research on emotional intelligence in leadership documented in Daniel Goleman, Emotional Intelligence: Why It Can Matter More Than IQ.

Chapter 3: Select the Right People

The high-performing asshole concept and its organizational dangers are based on author experience and validated through research. See Robert I. Sutton, The No Asshole Rule: Building a Civilized Workplace and Surviving One That Isn't.

The gatekeepers, Santas, and senseis evaluator framework was developed by John Dowd and the team at FORGE SOFware LLC, based on their extensive experience in military special operations selection processes.

Buy vs. build talent acquisition framework draws on both military special operations selection philosophy and business hiring research. See Claudio Fernandez-Araoz, It's Not the How or the What but the Who: Succeed by Surrounding Yourself with the Best (Harvard Business Review Press, 2014).

John Dowd's philosophy on selection emphasizing intelligence and adaptability is from author interview, The Debrief podcast, 2024. Dowd is a former Navy SEAL and founder of FORGE SOFware LLC.

Selection never stops concept reflects the continuous evaluation philosophy observed in elite units. The principle is documented across multiple author interviews with tactical commanders, 2023–2024.

Phil Hansen's insights on team collaboration are from author interview, The Debrief podcast, 2024. Hansen's experience in tactical leadership provides perspective on building collaborative environments under pressure.

Chapter 4: Embrace Strong People

Research on psychological safety in teams is foundational. See Amy Edmondson, The Fearless Organization: Creating Psychological Safety in the Workplace for Learning, Innovation, and Growth. Google's Project Aristotle findings are published at rework.withgoogle.com.

Bob Koonce, interview by Jon Becker, "Using Nuclear Submarine Culture to Create High Reliability Teams," The Debrief with Jon Becker, Battle Proven Leadership, Episode 1, 2024.

Gregg Popovich's leadership philosophy with the San Antonio Spurs demonstrates continuous improvement in action. His approach is documented in Jackie MacMullan, "The Coaching Genius of Gregg Popovich," ESPN.com; Wright Thompson, "The Secret of Spurs Culture," ESPN.com, 2019; David Aldridge, "Inside Popovich's Leadership," NBA.com, 2017.

Research on psychological safety in teams demonstrates its critical role in collaboration. See Edmondson, The Fearless Organization. Google's Project Aristotle research findings are available at rework.withgoogle.com/guides.

Chapter 5: Enforce High Standards

Billie Jean King's philosophy on pressure is documented in her book Pressure Is a Privilege: Lessons I've Learned from Life and the Battle of the Sexes. The title phrase encapsulates her approach to high-stakes competition.

Travis Kelce's sideline interaction with Coach Andy Reid during Super Bowl LVIII (February 11, 2024, Allegiant Stadium, Las Vegas) demonstrated emotional regulation under championship pressure. Kelce's post-game reflection and Reid's response are documented in multiple sources: "Kelce Apologizes for Sideline Moment," NFL.com, February 14, 2024; Tyler Dunne, "Inside the Kelce-Reid Super Bowl Moment," ESPN.com, February 14, 2024; "Reid Dismisses Kelce Incident," CNN Sports, February 12, 2024; Travis Kelce and Jason Kelce, New Heights podcast, episode 79, February 14, 2024.

Chapter 6: Collaborate Deliberately

AARDVARK Tactical was founded in 1986 and has served law enforcement and military special operations units for nearly four decades. The company's client relationships provided the author with unprecedented access to elite team operations and leadership practices.

Joe Bucchignano's insights on NYPD Emergency Service Unit (ESU) culture and expertise harvesting are from author interview, The Debrief podcast, episode 41: "Inside the NYPD Emergency Service Unit (ESU)." Bucchignano spent twenty years at ESU working in various assignments and provides perspective on how elite units intentionally cultivate diverse expertise and defer to local knowledge regardless of seniority.

Bill Kirst's insights on organizational change and grief are from author interview, The Debrief podcast, December 2024. Kirst is the host of the Coffee and Change podcast and has led corporate change initiatives for major technology companies. His framework connecting change to grief provides a psychological foundation for understanding team resistance to organizational shifts.

Mike Tyson's quote, "Everybody has plans until they get hit for the first time," was made in response to opponent Tyrell Biggs's claim to have a plan to beat him. In The Record (Hackensack, New Jersey, October 16, 1987, p. E3), "Champ Tyson faces doubters in first defense," by John Rowe.

Marc Polymeropoulos's CIA leadership principles are drawn from author interview, The Debrief podcast, 2024. See also Marc Polymeropoulos, Clarity in Crisis: Leadership Lessons from the CIA.

Boyd's OODA Loop (Observe-Orient-Decide-Act) with emphasis on orientation as the central element is from John R. Boyd, "The Essence of Winning and Losing" (unpublished briefing, 1995). See also Frans P.B. Osinga, Science, Strategy and War: The Strategic Theory of John Boyd.

Mark McGrath's explanation of Boyd's OODA framework is from author interview, The Debrief podcast, 2024. McGrath is a former Marine artillery officer and recognized expert on Boyd's work.

Chapter 7: Build a Decision Machine

Kevin Cyr's framework for decision authority distribution is from author interview, The Debrief podcast, 2024. Cyr commanded the RCMP Emergency Response Team.

The Lindt Café siege occurred on December 15–16, 2014, in Sydney, Australia. Ben Bessant's account of the tactical team's experience is from author interview, The Debrief podcast, 2024. The NSW State Coroner's inquest findings are documented in State Coroner of New South Wales, "Inquest into the deaths arising from the Lindt Café siege" (Sydney: State Coroner's Court of New South Wales, May 2017).

The song "Freewill" by Rush (Permanent Waves, Anthem Records, 1980), written by Neil Peart, expresses the idea that choosing not to decide is itself a decision.

Jeff Bezos's Type 1/Type 2 decision framework and the 70 percent information threshold is from his 2015 Letter to Shareholders, Amazon.com, Inc. (April 2016).

General Jim Mattis's observation on cultivating decisiveness is from Jim Mattis and Bing West, Call Sign Chaos: Learning to Lead (Random House, 2019).

The 70 percent decision threshold is advocated by Jeff Bezos, Kevin Cyr, and General Stanley McChrystal in Team of Teams: New Rules of Engagement for a Complex World (Portfolio, 2015).

The After-Action Review (AAR) methodology originated in the US Army. See US Army Field Manual 7-0, Training for Full Spectrum Operations (Washington, DC: Headquarters, Department of the Army, 2008). Organizational applications in Marilyn Darling, David Meador, and Shawn Patterson, "Cultivating a Learning Culture at the US Army," Harvard Business Review, July-August 2005.

Gary Klein's premortem technique is documented in Klein, "Performing a Project Premortem," Harvard Business Review, September 2007.

Chapter 8: Improve Continuously

The doorknob debrief story illustrates how informal feedback mechanisms can transform organizational learning. Based on author experience and tactical unit observations, 2024–2025.

Kaizen philosophy and its organizational applications are documented in Masaaki Imai, Kaizen: The Key to Japan's Competitive Success. See also Jeffrey K. Liker, The Toyota Way: 14 Management Principles from the World's Greatest Manufacturer.

John Montenegro, personal communication with the author, 2024.

Evolution, not revolution as an improvement philosophy emerged from author observations of elite unit continuous improvement programs and tactical commander interviews, 2023–2024.

Status quo is loss principle reflects the competitive reality that standing still means falling behind. The concept is supported by strategic management research. See Michael E. Porter, Competitive Strategy: Techniques for Analyzing Industries and Competitors (New York: Free Press, 1980).

Chapter 9: Take Risks and Embrace Failure

Gary Klein's cognitive debrief methodology is from Klein, Sources of Power: How People Make Decisions.

Jennifer Prohaska, interview by Jon Becker, "Tactical Longevity," The Debrief with Jon Becker, Episode 62, 2025. Prohaska is a clinical psychologist and founder of the Tactical Longevity anti-fragility training framework.

Dan Dworkis, interview by Jon Becker, "The Emergency Mind," The Debrief with Jon Becker, Episode 37, March 13, 2024. Dworkis is the chief medical officer of the Mission Critical Team Institute and author of The Emergency Mind: Wiring Your Brain for Performance Under Pressure (2021).

Conclusion: Putting It All Together

The return to Officer Louis Pompei's story in the conclusion connects the book's practical frameworks to their deeper purpose: protecting those who protect others.

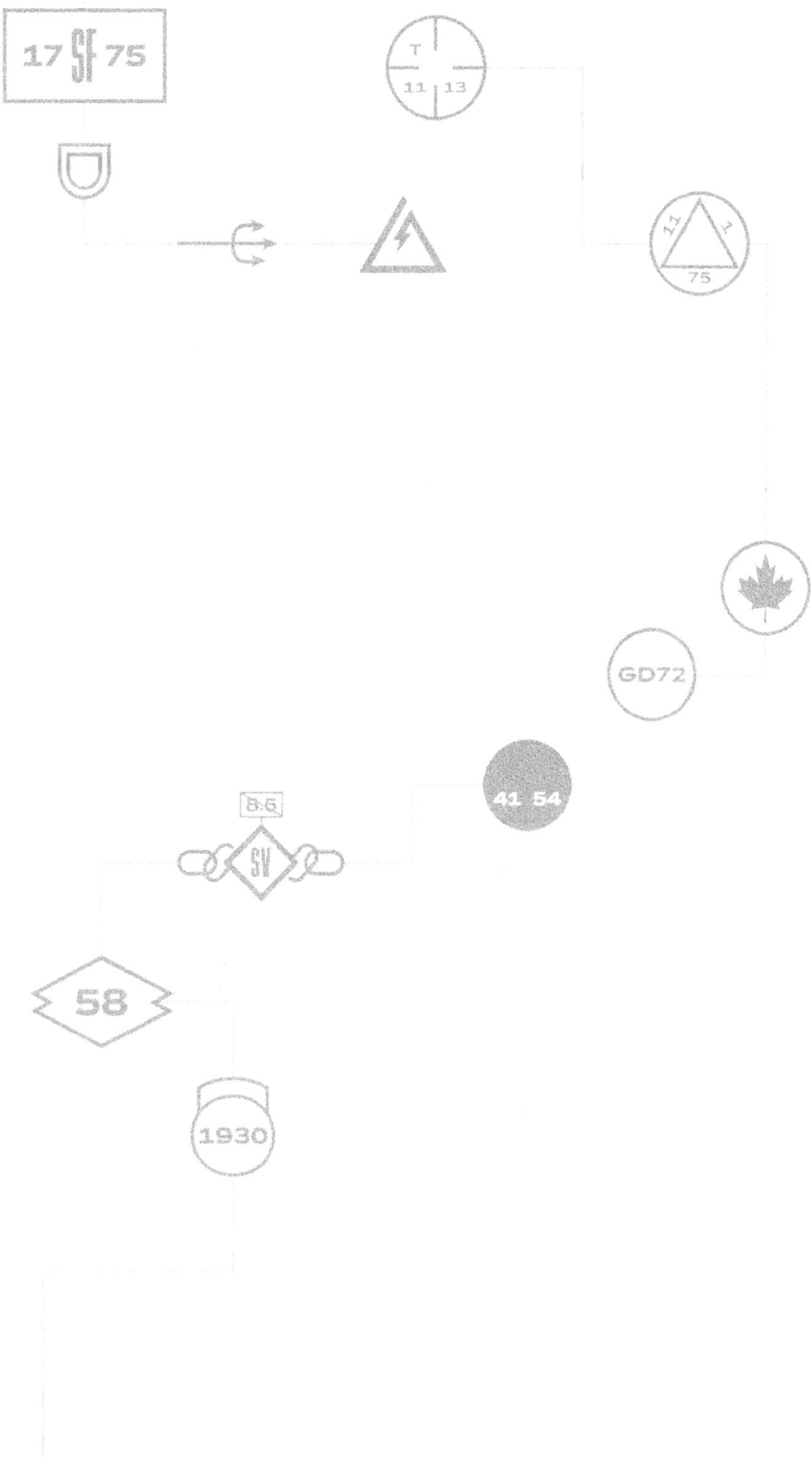
17 SF 75
T
11 13
11
1
75
GD72
41 54
8.5
SV
58
1930

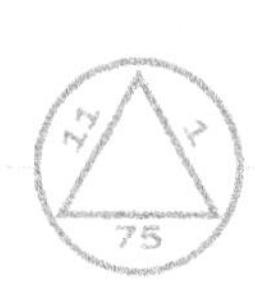

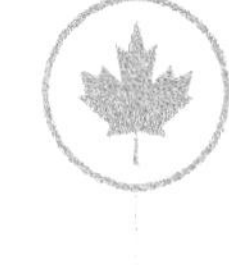

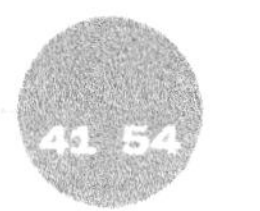

SELECTED BIBLIOGRAPHY

Books

Blaber, Pete. *The Mission, the Men, and Me: Lessons from a Former Delta Force Commander.* Dutton Caliber, 2010.

Brand, Stewart. *The Clock of the Long Now: Time and Responsibility.* Basic Books, 1999.

Coyle, Daniel. *The Culture Code: The Secrets of Highly Successful Groups.* Bantam Books, 2018.

Drucker, Peter F. *The Practice of Management.* Harper & Row, 1954.

Dweck, Carol. *Mindset: The New Psychology of Success.* Random House, 2006.

Edmondson, Amy. *The Fearless Organization: Creating Psychological Safety in the Workplace for Learning, Innovation, and Growth.* Wiley, 2018.

Ericsson, Anders, and Robert Pool. *Peak: Secrets from the New Science of Expertise.* Harper One, 2016.

Gerstner, Louis V. Jr. *Who Says Elephants Can't Dance? Leading a Great Enterprise Through Dramatic Change.* Harper Business, 2003.

Goleman, Daniel. *Emotional Intelligence: Why It Can Matter More Than IQ.* Bantam Books, 1998.

Greenleaf, Robert K. *Servant Leadership: A Journey into the Nature of Legitimate Power and Greatness.* Paulist Press, 2002.

Hastings, Reed, and Erin Meyer. *No Rules Rules: Netflix and the Culture of Reinvention.* Penguin Press, 2020.

Holiday, Ryan. *Ego Is the Enemy.* Portfolio, 2016.

Imai, Masaaki. *Kaizen: The Key to Japan's Competitive Success.* McGraw-Hill, 1986.

Isaacson, Walter. *Steve Jobs.* Simon & Schuster, 2011.

Kerr, James. *Legacy: What the All Blacks Can Teach Us About the Business of Life.* Constable, 2013.

King, Billie Jean, with Christine Brennan. *Pressure Is a Privilege: Lessons I've Learned from Life and the Battle of the Sexes.* LifeTime Media, 2008.

Klein, Gary. *Seeing What Others Don't: The Remarkable Ways We Gain Insights.* PublicAffairs, 2013.

Klein, Gary. *Sources of Power: How People Make Decisions.* MIT Press, 1998.

Klein, Gary. *Streetlights and Shadows: Searching for the Keys to Adaptive Decision Making.* Bradford Books, 2009.

Knight, Phil. *Shoe Dog: A Memoir by the Creator of Nike.* Scribner, 2016.

Liker, Jeffrey K. *The Toyota Way: 14 Management Principles from the World's Greatest Manufacturer.* McGraw-Hill, 2004.

Osinga, Frans P.B. *Science, Strategy and War: The Strategic Theory of John Boyd.* Routledge, 2006.

Polymeropoulos, Marc. *Clarity in Crisis: Leadership Lessons from the CIA.* Harper Business, 2021.

Schein, Edgar H., with Peter Schein. *Organizational Culture and Leadership.* 5th ed. Jossey-Bass, 2016.

Schein, Edgar H., and Peter A. Schein. *Humble Leadership: The Power of Relationships, Openness, and Trust.* Berrett-Koehler, 2023.

Sinek, Simon. *Leaders Eat Last: Why Some Teams Pull Together and Others Don't.* Portfolio, 2017.

Sinek, Simon. *Start With Why: How Great Leaders Inspire Everyone to Take Action.* Portfolio, 2011.

Stone, Brad. *The Everything Store: Jeff Bezos and the Age of Amazon.* Little, Brown, 2013.

Taleb, Nassim Nicholas. *Antifragile: Things That Gain from Disorder.* Random House, 2012.

Willink, Jocko, and Leif Babin. *Extreme Ownership: How U.S. Navy SEALs Lead and Win.* St. Martin's Press, 2017.

Zak, Paul J. *Trust Factor: The Science of Creating High-Performance Companies*. AMACOM, 2017.

Academic Articles and Studies

Klein, Gary. "Performing a Project Premortem." *Harvard Business Review,* September 2007.

Zak, Paul J. "The Neuroscience of Trust." *Harvard Business Review,* January–February 2017.

Interviews and Primary Sources

The following individuals were interviewed by the author for *The Debrief* podcast, 2023–2025, and their insights were used in this book:

- Ben Bessant, NSW TOU (Ret.)
- Col. Pete Blaber, former Delta Force Commander
- Joe Bucchignano, NYPD Emergency Service Unit (Ret.)
- Insp. Kevin Cyr, RCMP Emergency Response Team Commander
- John Dowd, FORGE SOFware, LLC
- Chief Phil Hansen
- Cmdr. Sid Heal
- Chief Mike Hillmann, former LAPD SWAT
- James Kerr, author of *Legacy*
- Bob Koonce, US Navy (ret.)
- Michael Lumpkin, US Navy (ret.) and former ASD-SOLIC
- Mark McGrath, OODA Loop and Boyd Scholar
- Lt. Lee McMillion, LAPD D-Platoon (SWAT)
- Chief John Perez, Pasadena PD (ret.)
- Marc Polymeropoulos, former CIA Senior Intelligence Officer
- Jennifer Prohaska, PhD, high-performance psychologist

Additional interviews were conducted with tactical personnel who required anonymity due to current or past assignments in these organizations.

- BRI (Brigade de Recherche et d'Intervention) team leader who participated in the November 13, 2015, Paris attacks response
- Delta Norge, Norway
- FBI–HRT
- Team Diane, DSU, Belgium
- US Air Force
- US Army
- US Navy

GLOSSARY

70 percent Rule

A decision-making teaching principle that waiting for complete certainty leads to paralysis. When you have approximately 70 percent of the information needed, it's time to decide. Associated with Kevin Cyr and Charles "Sid" Heal. See also: satisficing.

Accountability (Three-Way Street)

The principle that accountability flows in three directions: upward (to leadership), downward (to those you lead), and sideways (to peers). Elite organizations maintain accountability at all three levels simultaneously. Peer accountability is often the most powerful form.

Andon Cord

Toyota's system allows any worker to stop the production line when problems are detected. Represents the principle that every team member has authority to halt operations to address quality issues. Contrast with Ford's system where only supervisors could stop the line. Foundational to Kaizen culture.

Bar Raiser

Amazon's system of specially trained employee volunteers who serve as objective third-party assessors during hiring. Bar Raisers undergo six to twelve months of preparation, sit in on interview panels for teams other than their own, and have veto power over hiring decisions. Their singular question: Will this person raise the bar? Essentially a sensei factory.

Brain Trust

Pixar's system of peer review for creative work, characterized by frank, candid feedback given without authority. The creative team retains full ownership while receiving unfiltered input from peers allowing problems to be addressed without politics or posturing.

Buy vs. Build

A selection framework for determining what qualities candidates must already possess (buy) versus what can be developed through training (build). Technical skills typically live in the build column, character lives in the buy column. There is no training program that installs integrity.

Candor Without Cruelty

The practice of providing direct, honest feedback is rooted in genuine care for the person's development. Distinguished from being merely "nice" (which avoids discomfort) versus being "kind" (which serves the person's genuine interest even when uncomfortable). Direct, candid feedback sharpens the organization's knives through friction.

Cathedral Thinking

The mindset of building something greater than oneself, something that will outlast one's tenure. Derived from medieval cathedral builders who began projects they knew they would never see completed. Leaders who build cathedrals create lasting value rather than personal monuments.

Choosing the Chooser

The principle that decision authority should flow to whoever possesses three traits: the training to understand the problem, the situational awareness to see what is actually happening, and the time to make the call before the window closes. Often requires pushing decision authority down to the person closest to the problem.

Community Devotion

One of three selection criteria categories (alongside individual performance and team impact). Measures a candidate's commitment to organizational values over personal gain. Essential for identifying people who prioritize mission over self-interest.

Compound Effect

The principle that small improvements consistently applied over time, compound into extraordinary results. The accumulation of countless small acts done right creates elite performance. Related to Kaizen and "evolutions not revolutions."

The Crucible

The Marine Corps' fifty-four-hour final test where recruits travel forty-eight miles, complete twenty-nine problem-solving exercises, survive on three MREs, and operate on minimal sleep. Each obstacle station bears the name of a Marine hero. Culminates in receiving the Eagle, Globe, and Anchor from their drill instructor. Designed for cultural transformation through shared hardship.

Cultural Indoctrination

Deliberate systems for transmitting organizational culture to new members. Every organization indoctrinates its members; the only question is whether intentionally or accidentally. Examples include the Marine Corps Crucible and Disney's Traditions program.

Culture as Operating System

The central metaphor of the book. Like a computer's operating system, culture runs in the background, invisible to most users but determining everything they experience. It manages resources, handles conflicts, enables information flow, and determines whether initiatives thrive or crash. Culture isn't just one aspect of the game; it is the game.

Culture Drift

The gradual erosion of standards that occurs when enforcement lapses. Culture never stands still; if it is not actively defended, it decays toward convenience and comfort. Happens incrementally, not suddenly. Once you get complacent, you set a new baseline, and it happens over and over again until you're somewhere you don't want to be. Related to Broken Windows Theory and Leadership Is Gardening.

Debrief/After-Action Review (AAR)

Structured review of operations focused on uncovering truth: What actually happened? What did we miss? How do we get better? Elite organizations focus on process and orientation accuracy. The goal is measuring the accuracy of orientation to reality, then improving everything that didn't go as expected.

Decision Inertia

The trap where the absence of disaster is interpreted as evidence that current inaction is working. Each hour that passes without catastrophe makes it harder to justify action, even as circumstances deteriorate. Demonstrated in the Lindt Café siege where commanders interpreted hostage escapes as success rather than warning signs.

Decision Machine

Systems that convert collective wisdom into decisive action when time is short, information is incomplete, and stakes are high. Combines proper orientation, appropriate decision authority placement, and acceptance that perfect information is rarely available.

Define the Prince

Before selection begins, clearly define what you're looking for in behavioral terms. Converting abstract qualities (team player) into specific, observable behaviors. Derived from the fairy tale principle: You have to know what your prince looks like before you start kissing frogs.

Deliberate Action (DA)

In tactical operations, a planned entry executed on the team's terms, using training, tactics, and the element of surprise. Contrasted with Emergency Action, which is reactive.

Don't Be the Emperor

Reference to "The Emperor's New Clothes" fable. Leaders must create conditions where people feel safe telling them uncomfortable truths. A hierarchy that prevents truth from reaching decision-makers kills the organization's ability to adapt. The most valuable person is often the one willing to tell you that you're wrong.

Ego Is the Enemy

The principle that ego creates blind spots, prevents learning, breeds overconfidence, and leads to fatal mistakes. Ego is a problem at three phases: aspiration (makes us talk instead of work), success (blinds us to others' contributions), and failure (prevents learning). Confidence is earned; ego is stolen.

Elite

Not a descriptor of talent alone, but of behavior, standards, and sustained performance over time. Elite teams are not defined by who they attract, but by what they tolerate and enforce. Elite is earned through relentless commitment to improvement, accountability, and the cultural practices that produce consistent excellence.

Emergency Action (EA)

In tactical operations, a reactive entry triggered by immediate threat to life. The team loses initiative and must respond to circumstances dictated by the adversary. Contrasted with deliberate action.

Fixed Mindset

The belief that abilities are static. People with fixed mindsets avoid challenges that might expose inadequacy, interpret effort as evidence of low ability, and see failure as a reflection of fundamental worth. Organizations with fixed mindsets protect current methods, interpret problems as threats, and punish failure. Contrast with growth mindset.

Gatekeeper (Evaluator Type)

One of three evaluator archetypes developed by John Dowd and FORGE SOFware, LLC. The bitter veteran with impossibly high standards who underselects because admitting anyone means admitting someone could meet their standards. Takes pride in rejection rates. Produces false negatives. Should be restricted to objective, quantitative measurements. See also: Santa and sensei types.

Golden Circle

Simon Sinek's framework placing WHY at the center, surrounded by HOW, then WHAT. Most organizations communicate from outside in (what they do, then how, then maybe why). Inspiring organizations reverse this, starting with why. Your people work for your purpose, which becomes their purpose.

Ground Truth

The actual reality of a situation, as distinguished from reports, assumptions, or filtered information. Leaders must actively hunt for ground truth by bypassing hierarchical filters that tend to sanitize information. The map is not the territory. See also: Orientation.

Growth Mindset

The belief that abilities can be developed. People with growth mindsets embrace challenges, view effort as the path to mastery, and treat failure as information about what to work on next. Organizations with growth mindsets welcome problems as opportunities, expect methods can always improve, and treat failure as learning. Contrast with fixed mindset.

High-Performing Asshole (HPA)

A high performer who is selfish, narcissistic, and toxic to team culture. HPAs win by making others lose. The ideal selection isn't just about hiring high performers; it's about avoiding high performers who destroy team chemistry despite individual competence. One HPA can contaminate an entire organization.

Humble Leadership

Leadership is characterized by humility rather than ego. Real strength isn't arrogance; it's the ability to be strong enough to be humble. Humility allows learning, adaptation, and acceptance of feedback. Arrogance is the armor that keeps reality at bay.

Individual Performance

One of three selection criteria categories (alongside team impact and community devotion). What people achieve on their own. The easiest to measure and most frequently overmeasured. High individual performance does not guarantee positive team contribution.

Inspected vs. Expected

The principle is that people do what is inspected, not what is expected. You can expect excellence all day long, but unless you actually measure, verify, and hold people accountable, your expectations are just wishes. What you permit defines who you are, not what you articulate.

Junior Speaks First

The practice of having the most junior person share their assessment before senior members in planning sessions or debriefs. Prevents hierarchy from anchoring discussion and silencing good ideas. Once a senior person speaks, juniors tend to defer or conform rather than offer independent perspective.

Kaizen

Japanese term literally meaning "good change." The relentless, daily, never-satisfied pursuit of getting a little bit better at something that matters. Not continuous improvement as a program but as a way of life. The operating system is constantly being upgraded. Toyota's Andon cord system exemplifies kaizen culture.

Keeper Test

Netflix's selection principle: Would you fight to keep this person? If not, they probably shouldn't be on the team. Applied during layoffs that led to Netflix's foundational insight about talent density.

Leaders Eat Last

The servant leadership principle is that leaders prioritize their team's needs before their own. Derived from military tradition where officers ensure troops are fed before taking their own meal. Builds trust and demonstrates that leadership is about service, not privilege.

Leadership Is Gardening

The metaphor is that leaders cultivate conditions for growth rather than commanding outcomes. Gardeners don't make plants grow; they create conditions where growth happens naturally. Includes defending the garden against threats, weeds, and the gradual drift that happens when inspection lapses.

Murder Your Own Ideas

The practice of attacking your own strategies and plans to expose weaknesses before reality does. Related to red teaming. The goal isn't for any individual to be "right" but for the team to collectively find the best solution. Requires dropping ego and embracing disagreement.

OODA Loop

John Boyd's framework: Observe, Orient, Decide, Act. Commonly misunderstood as a speed competition. In Boyd's actual conception, orientation is the largest component and central position— not one step among four but the primary factor that matters. Orientation is a human's cognitive operating system that shapes what we notice, value, believe, and think is possible.

Orientation

The central and most important element of Boyd's OODA Loop. Your orientation is driven by genetic heritage, cultural traditions, previous experiences, new information, and analytical/synthetic capabilities. It can be both your greatest asset (enabling pattern recognition) and your fatal weakness (creating blind spots to novel situations). Achieving and sharing orientation must be part of your culture.

Own the Loss, Share the Win

The leadership principle that leaders take personal responsibility for failures while redirecting credit for successes to the team. When things go wrong, the response is this: "What could I have done differently?" not "Whose fault was this?" When things go well, "we" dominates the vocabulary.

Own the Yardstick

Taking control of evaluation standards rather than defaulting to convenient metrics. Requires investing in harder qualitative assessment because that's where the real signal lives. Organizations naturally drift toward measuring what's easy to measure, overweighting technical skills, and underweighting team contribution.

Peer Accountability

Accountability that flows sideways between teammates, often the most powerful form. When team members hold each other to standards, enforcement becomes distributed rather than dependent on leadership. Creates environments where "If you see something, say something" applies to performance and behavior, not just safety. The glue that maintains standards when no supervisor is watching.

Power Distance

Cultural measure of how readily subordinates question superiors. High positions of power can create distance in cultures (like

Korean Air before their reforms) and produce environments where subordinates cannot challenge authority, even when lives are at stake. Low-power distance enables truth to reach decision-makers.

Premortem

Gary Klein's technique of imagining a project has failed and working backward to identify what could have caused the failure. Conducted before execution (unlike a postmortem). Particularly valuable when confidence exceeds 90 percent, which is often when hubris creates blind spots.

Process Monkey

Marc Polymeropoulos's term for someone who asks: Have we checked all our boxes? What are we missing? Who has not been heard from? What assumptions might be wrong? In many organizations, this person is seen as an obstacle. In elite organizations, they're recognized as essential.

Psychological Safety

The shared belief that the team is safe for interpersonal risk-taking. Google's Project Aristotle identified it as the single most important factor in team effectiveness. Who is on a team matters less than how team members interact. People must feel safe to speak up, share ideas, and admit mistakes.

Qualitative vs. Quantitative Assessment

Quantitative assessments can be counted, timed, or measured without judgment (pushups, test scores, credentials). Qualitative assessments require evaluator judgment (leadership, teamwork, composure). The most important selection criteria are qualitative, while the easiest things to measure are quantitative.

Questioning Attitude

The cultural expectation that team members question decisions, assumptions, and plans rather than simply accept them. Distinguished from insubordination, questioning is expected as part of collaboration. Related to Don't Be the Emperor and psychological safety.

Rank-Off Planning

The practice of removing rank from planning discussions so that the best idea wins regardless of source. Information has more rank than the person carrying it. When hierarchy dominates planning, junior insights are suppressed and senior assumptions go unchallenged.

Red Team

A group of objective people, not part of the original planning, brought in to serve as an opposing force. The goal is to expose weaknesses before actual execution. Goes beyond playing devil's advocate to full-scale intellectual combat aimed at exposing every vulnerability.

Santa (Evaluator Type)

One of three evaluator archetypes developed by John Dowd and FORGE SOFware, LLC. Too lenient, too quick to see potential, too reluctant to deliver negative news. Overselects because saying no feels mean. Focuses on what candidates could become rather than what they are. Produces false positives. Should be restricted to objective, quantitative measurements. See also: gatekeeper and sensei types.

Satisficing

Decision science term for accepting a satisfactory solution rather than searching for the optimal one. Appropriate when time is limited and information is incomplete. Waiting for the perfect answer while acceptable answers pass you by is not prudence; it is abdication. See also: 70 percent rule.

Selection Never Stops

The principle that selection is not a one-time event but an ongoing process. The qualities that got someone onto the team must continue to be demonstrated. Selection continues through every training evolution, every operation, every interaction. Standards that stop being enforced stop being standards.

Selfless Team

A team characterized by concern for others over self-interest. "Take care of the man next to you better than yourself." When ego dies, concern for others grows in its place. The foundation for truly elite performance.

Sensei (Evaluator Type)

The gold standard among evaluator archetypes developed by John Dowd and FORGE SOFware, LLC. Rigorous but developmental, demanding but fair. Motivated to find the right candidates, not to reject or accept everyone. Can deliver hard truths with respect. Understands that high standards and human decency aren't in conflict. Should be the only evaluators with votes on cultural fit. See also: gatekeeper and Santa types.

Servant Leadership

Leadership philosophy where the leader's primary role is to serve those they lead. Characterized by eating last, owning losses while sharing wins, finding paths forward for the team, and being remembered for how you made people feel. Contrasted with hierarchical leadership that prioritizes status and control.

Status Quo Is Getting Fat

The principle that there is no true status quo in competitive environments. Standing still while everyone else improves means falling behind. Like physical fitness, if you're not getting on the scale and actively maintaining, you're probably declining. Not improving is losing by default.

Talent Density

Netflix's concept that overall team performance depends on the concentration of high performers. Their foundational insight from 2001 layoffs: keeping only eighty highest performers with fewer people actually increased overall capability. Higher talent density produces better culture and better results.

Team Impact

One of three selection criteria categories (alongside individual performance and community devotion). How a person affects the people around them. The hardest to measure and most frequently ignored, but matters most. Google's Project Oxygen found that of eight behaviors that mattered for manager effectiveness, technical expertise ranked lowest; team impact ranked highest.

Type 1 vs. Type 2 Decisions

Jeff Bezos's framework. Type 1 decisions are consequential and irreversible (one-way doors) requiring methodical deliberation. Type 2 decisions are changeable and reversible (two-way doors) that can be made quickly. Most organizations mistakenly treat Type 2 decisions like Type 1, creating unnecessary slowness.

Wisdom of the Crowd

The principle that collective intelligence exceeds individual intelligence when properly harvested. The smartest person in the room is never one person; it is the room itself. Requires creating conditions where diverse perspectives are heard and the best idea wins regardless of source.

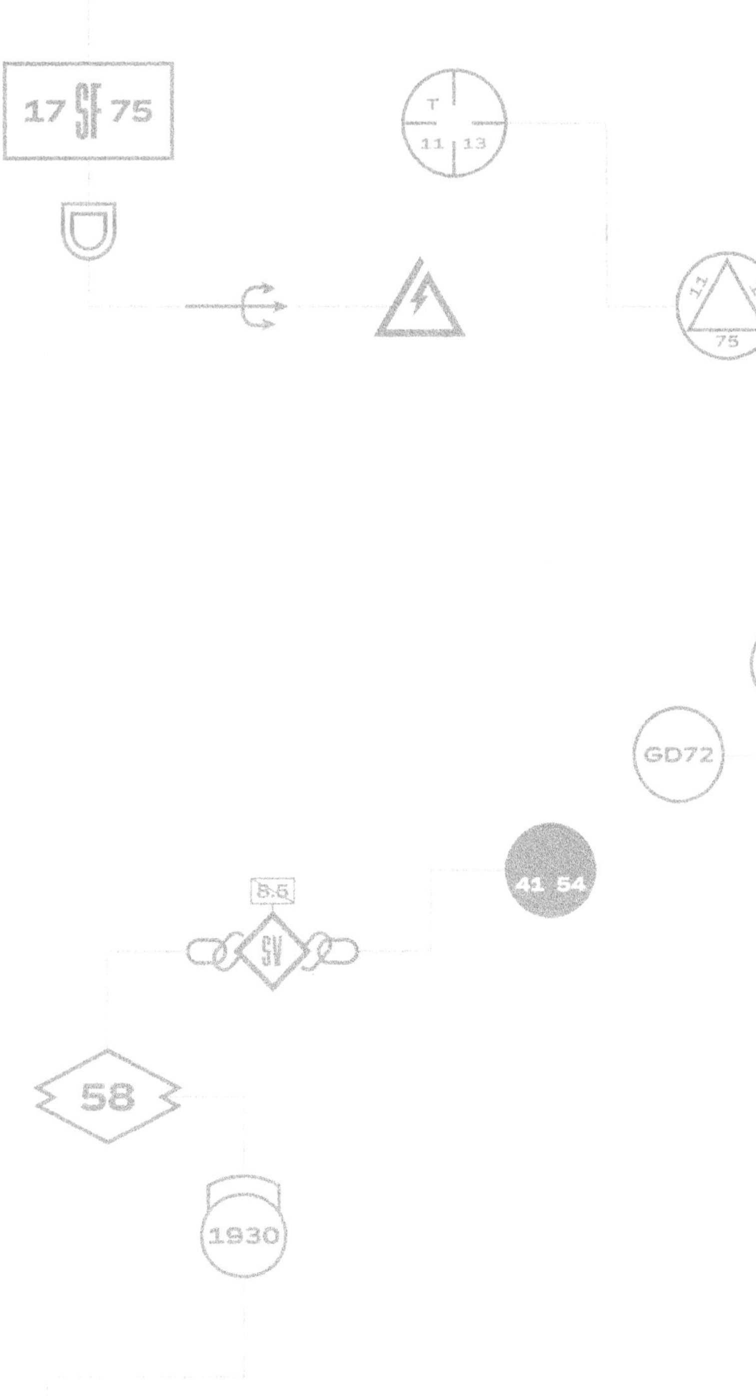

ACKNOWLEDGMENTS

My Family—There is no way this book ever gets finished without the patience and support of my family. Thank you for letting me pursue this dream at your expense. Thank you for reading and rereading. Thank you for listening to me drone on about nerdy culture stuff that you were not interested in. And most of all thank you for your love and support. I am so grateful for you and proud to call you guys my family.

Judy L Becker—I would be remiss if I didn't thank my late mom here. She made a lot of sacrifices for me, for my education and to grow my intellectual curiosity. Times like this are when I really miss her!

Mentors

Sid Heal—It is impossible to put into a note the effect Sid had on my life and thinking. It will have to suffice to say that who I am today was largely shaped by Sid's influence. He was the first one in the elite tactical community to take me under his wing and allow me to stand in his shadow. More than thirty years of friendship followed, for which I am profoundly grateful. If we are lucky, we meet one man like Sid in our lives. If we are really lucky, we get to call him our friend. I miss him every day.

John Kolman—Founder of the National Tactical Officers Association, John had a profound impact on the tactical community worldwide. He was a visionary who saw something no one else did and made it happen. John's mentorship early in my career and nurturing of my writing skills is part of the reason this book exists. I am grateful for his friendship.

Tim Anderson—USMC O6 and LAPD Sergeant, an amazing fusion thinker who took the USMC doctrine and made it applicable to street cops. Tim was like the interpreter for Sid who made everything Sid talked about somehow sound easy. *The Debrief* is a direct result of Tim's death. I have never seen anyone suffer such physical adversity with more grace. A great man who is sorely missed.

Phil Hansen—Possibly the finest man any of us will ever know. Phil is a legend who is so generous with his time, kind and caring, that it truly inspires everyone he knows to just be better.

Mike Hillmann—Like a tactical stepdad to me, Mike has taught me more over coffee than I can possibly explain. Very few men have the amazing reputation and knowledge he has. Truly Mike has had a profound impact on who I am and how I think. Forever grateful.

Ron McCarthy—No one changed my thinking on armor the way Ron McCarthy did. Project 7 exists because of Ron, and I feel his influence on me every day. Ron may be the only D-Platoon member who saved more people *after* he retired. Grateful for twenty+ years of friendship and miss him.

RK Miller—Humble, kind, understated but so dedicated, caring, and compassionate. Thank you for your thirty years of friendship and mentorship. I am hereby officially forgiving you for trying to light the library on fire during one of my classes and accusing me of cheating for winning the MP5 shoot off.

This Book's Red Team and My Friends

Kevin Cyr—The commanding general of this red team. Simply one of the smartest dudes I have ever known. Kevin and I have a way of arguing about everything in the most recreational way possible. His work on decision-making, incident command, team building, and other topics has shaped my thinking for the better. This book is a much better work because he poured his soul into sharpening it and me.

Stan Coerr—Marine officer, Cobra pilot, scholar, author. You name it, he has done it. Truly a brilliant scholar who made this book dramatically better with his editing. Grateful is the only word I have.

Toby Darby—For his constant help and guidance and for always being ready for a good argument. A wonderful human being and a great friend and teaching partner

Josh Wofford—For editing the document, giving me great ideas, and always making me smarter every time we are together.

Friends

JW "Max" Dieter—We are a safer country because of you. I am a better man because of our friendship. There are a lot of people still alive because of sacrifices that you and your team have made. Thank you.

Brian Driscoll—Truly a man of honor. There are very few men in the world who would have had the integrity to do what Drizz did, and it cost him his career with the FBI. "I regret nothing" is the best line I've ever seen in a farewell email. Grateful to be his friend and thankful for the sacrifices he made on our behalf.

Michael Lumpkin—Served our country in more ways than I can count. He has a perspective on government and leadership that is unique and is unbelievably generous with his time, knowledge, and friendship.

Jordan MacWilliams—I am grateful for my friendship with him and so profoundly impressed by his resilience and humility. Thank you for letting me share your story.

Lee McMillion—My brother from a different mother. Lee is one of the best humans I know and makes me better every time I am with him. I have never met anyone with more reason to be arrogant and less ability to do that.

Guests on The Debrief with Jon Becker Podcast

Pete Blaber—A legend in the special operations world who has been at the center of almost every conflict in the past twenty-five years. His work *The Mission, the Men, and Me* is simply exceptional.

Joe Bucchignano—Twenty years at NYPD ESU taught Joe things about teamwork that most people never learn. His perspective on harvesting diverse expertise and deferring to the person closest to the problem fundamentally shaped how I think about collaboration.

Dan Dworkis—Dan is an amazing doctor but a more amazing scholar, who helped to reshape the way I viewed critical incident decisions, teamwork, and most importantly how I viewed failure.

Gary Klein—Rarely do you get to interview a legend and truly learn from the master. Gary's work is the basis for everything that has followed in decision science, and I am grateful for his time.

Bob Koonce—My submariner friend. Trip wires and questioning everything are part of my lexicon because of Bob.

Mark McGrath—Absolutely the smartest guy I've ever met about John Boyd's work. Mark is a deep thinker who has spent a great deal of time understanding how we make decisions. Completely transformed the way I see Boyd and orientation. Mark weighs heavily in the decision chapters in this book. He is also apparently a savant at recognizing movie locations from the 1960s.

Marc Polymeropoulos—A great thinker who spent a lot of time doing hidden stuff to keep us safe. The process monkey and glue guy now live in my head rent free.

Jenny Prohaska—For being the most practical and plain-spoken police psychologist I have ever known. Jenny has a way of telling you your feelings really matter and saying fuck your feelings in the same sentence and it makes sense! What a gift you are.

Organizations

NTOA—My relationship with the National Tactical Officers Association dates back to the mid-1990's when John Kolman made me a member when no one outside of sworn law enforcement—like me—did so. In the thirty plus years that have followed, the NTOA has done amazing work, and I have been privileged to play a small part in that. NTOA is the reason I started writing and I will forever be in debt. I would also like to specifically acknowledge Thor Eells, Don Kester, Mary Hines, Corey Lubey, and Steve Mescan for their mentorship, guidance, and friendship over the years.

CATO SLP Classes 1-4—Working on the CATO Strategic Leadership Program has truly been one of the most rewarding experiences of my life. The men who have completed this program are truly amazing leaders who are making a difference every day to the men and women they work with. It is not an overstatement to say that this program has transformed me as much as it has the students. Much of this book comes from SLP.

SOFware LLC (John Dowd and Aaron Rife)—For teaching me almost everything I know about elite unit selection from a technical standpoint. These guys are doing revolutionary work, and I am profoundly grateful to be friends with them and to have a chance to learn from them. And of course, commit acts of jackassery together to the disappointment of the adults in every room we haunt.

AARDVARK Tactical—I am grateful to my team at AARDVARK and all the people who have been a part of our team over the years. I have been gifted with a core team that has been with me for twenty+ years. We literally grew up together. They make me better every day, and our work together gives my life purpose.

Units and Teams

It is impossible to thank all the units and teams I have worked with over the years and that helped to shape my development. I have been allowed into places I should have never been; snuck onto helicopters; taken out on boats; driven in armored vehicles; taken on ops; worked into training scenarios; allowed to shoot on unit ranges; and blown stuff up that no civilian has a right to do. I am profoundly grateful to this community for the life it has given me and the knowledge it has shared. I hope I have been able to return even a small part of the kindness you have shown me over the years.

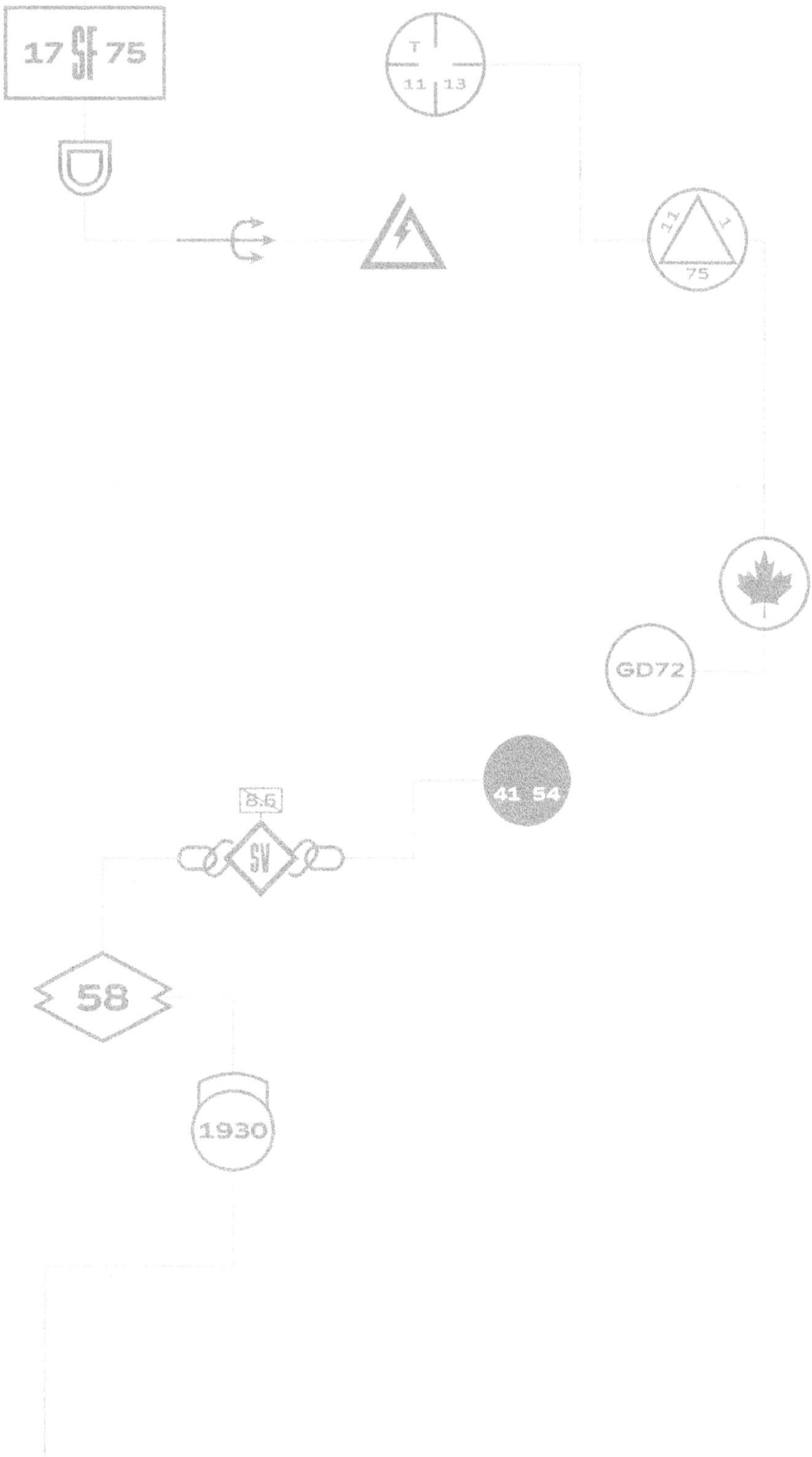
17 SF 75
T
11 13
11
1
75
GD72
41 54
8.6
SV
58
1930

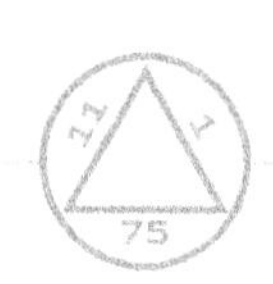

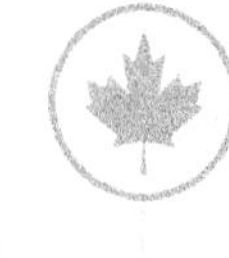

ABOUT THE AUTHOR

JON B. BECKER has spent four decades at the intersection of elite tactical operations and business leadership. At seventeen, he launched AARDVARK Tactical from a desk in his mother's den. What began as a small climbing-gear business evolved into one of the world's premier tactical equipment companies. He is also the creator of Project 7, a top of market tactical body armor brand.

He is a TEDx speaker and is also a frequent keynote speaker for agencies and conferences nationwide. He is a recipient of the Spirit of the NTOA Award from the National Tactical Officers Association.

Becker's articles have appeared in *Entrepreneur, Jane's International Defence Review, the Loyola of Los Angeles Entertainment Law Journal, CATO News, Officer, POLICE, The Tactical Edge, and Police and Security News*. He writes a quarterly "Lessons Learned from The Debrief" column for *Tactical Edge* magazine.

Becker hosts *The Debrief with Jon Becker*, now in its seventh season with more than 1.5 million views and listens and ranked among the top government podcasts worldwide. A documentary filmmaker, Becker directed *Confronting Hate: Responding to the Tree of Life Attack and Priority of Life*.

Becker holds a Juris Doctor degree from Loyola of Los Angeles Law School, a BA in Philosophy from CSULA, and is an attorney admitted to practice in California. He lives in Los Angeles with his wife of 36 years, Melissa and their two children. He also enjoys ultradistance athletics and is a 5x time Ironman triathlete.

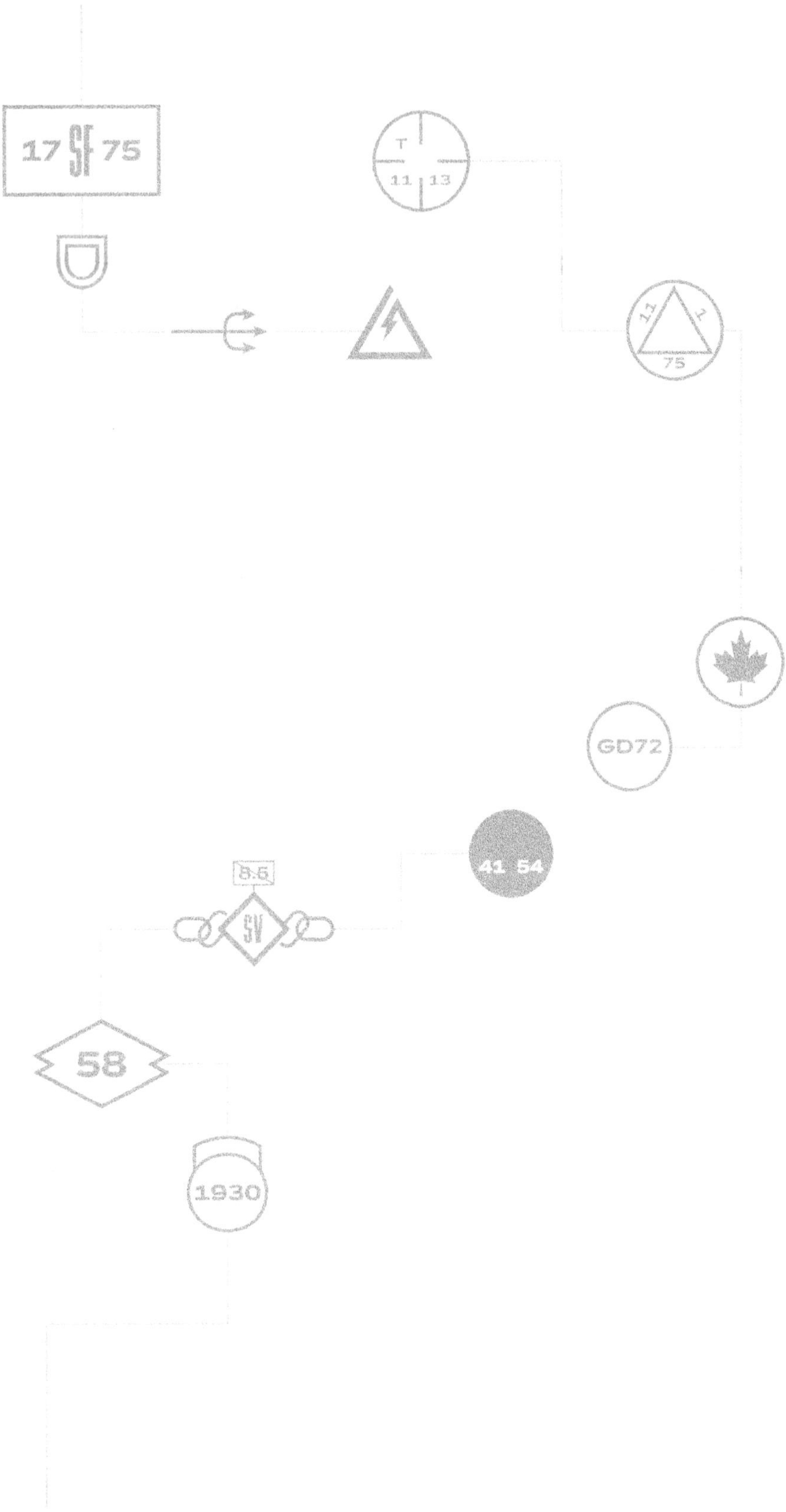
17 SF 75
T
11 13
11 1
75
GD72
41 54
8.5
SV
58
1930

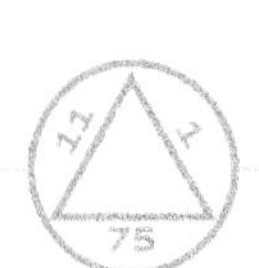

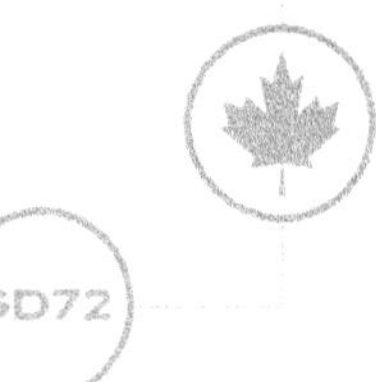

— RICH DIVINEY

Bestselling Author of Masters of Uncertainty
and Retired Navy SEAL CDR

"As a former tactical operator, senior member of government, and business executive, I can attest that Jon Becker nails it in his understanding that organizational culture is the operating system that drives the success or failure of any organization. His use of real-life examples in both tactical no-fail missions as well as the business world demonstrates that it is central to every organization regardless of mission. As he highlights...everyone is the keeper of the standards, so the standards must be clear, well-known, and non-negotiable.

Mr. Becker expertly uses his vast experience to make his argument with passion and delivers a 'must read' for every person in every organization that strives for successful outcomes."

— MICHAEL LUMPKIN

*US Navy SEAL (Ret.), Former Assistant Secretary of Defense,
Special Operations and Low Intensity Conflict,
Former Corporate President and CEO*

"Want your business to succeed? Want to build best teams? Want to be known as a great Leader? Build a great culture. In this book Jon Becker shows you how by sharing great stories that tell you why. A must read for all common sense leaders."

— PETE BLABER

Former Special Mission Unit Commander, Author of
The Mission, the Men, & Me *and* Common Sense Leadership

"The 9 Practices are not just catch-phrases for this book. They are how Jon Becker has built, sustains, and leads his private business, and the reason we have him present Culture Centric

Leadership to our entire team. Jon is extraordinarily credible on building a high-performing team, grounded in individual leadership and selflessness, promoting a culture where innovation thrives, and motives are focused on team success."

— LT. LEE MCMILLION

Commander, LAPD D-Platoon (SWAT)

"With more than 30 years personally involved in law enforcement tactical operations—as an operator, leader, and instructor—I've always been driven by one question: what truly sets apart those who succeed in this demanding profession? Over the years I've read extensively about leadership and team dynamics, but the guidance often felt scattered and incomplete.

In *Culture First*, Jon Becker brings it all together. He clearly identifies the traits that matter most for both individual performance and collective success. The principles are practical, direct, and rooted in the kind of mindset required for real-world service.

If you are serious about success and committed to genuine selfless service, this book is must-read. Everything you need is here. The only thing it can't provide is your personal determination and dedication. Knowing that, it's time to get to work."

— K. THOR EELLS

Executive Director, National Tactical Officers Association

"Jon Becker is a national treasure. He'll tell you that he's been serving elite units within law enforcement and the military for 40 years, but that undersells it—he's been shaping them. They know what I know: when you have a leadership or culture challenge your first call is to Jon.

In *Culture First*, Jon lays out nine essential practices about leadership and culture building. They are practical, hard-won, and immediately applicable.

Read this book. Put each chapter into practice."

— JOHN DOWD

SOFware / Selection Expert

"Jon Becker has carefully distilled decades of first-hand research, business experience, and exposure to elite tactical teams to produce a leadership and culture-building narrative that is entertaining, accurate, and most critically, actionable. Jon's outside sources are unimpeachable, and his personal insights are spot-on! This book belongs on every serious leader's desk or nightstand."

— PHIL HANSEN

Chief of Police (Ret.) and Director Emeritus,
National Tactical Officers Association

"I spent nearly twenty years on a SWAT team and three decades in law enforcement. After teaching critical incident leadership across the country, one truth keeps showing up: most operational failures aren't tactical problems — they're culture problems.

Culture First: The 9 Leadership Practices That Build Elite Teams explains why.

This book doesn't deal in slogans or motivational leadership clichés. It breaks down the practical leadership behaviors that create trust, ownership, loyalty, accountability, and genuine team cohesion — the things every elite unit depends on long before a crisis ever happens. The principles outlined here are the same ones missing in organizations that struggle with hesitation, internal friction, and lack of initiative.

I wish I had this book when I was a young SWAT sergeant. It would have saved years of trial-and-error learning and helped me build stronger teams faster.

Whether you lead a police department, specialized unit, organization, or hope to step into leadership one day, this book gives you the foundation every successful team stands on: culture. Without it, tactics fail. With it, ordinary groups become elite teams.

This isn't just leadership theory — it's the blueprint for building a team people trust when it matters most."

"If you lead people and care about the future of your organization, this book belongs on your desk. Culture can quietly undermine performance—or it can become the accelerant that drives sustained success. The difference is choice. And Jon Becker shows you, step by step, how to build it."

"For those like me who strongly believe the 'operationalization' of Leadership and Culture is critical to success, Jon's book is a fresh look at what it takes to lead through culture intentionally. Many academics love to theorize about 'norms and behaviors' with abstract concepts. But those of us in the trenches of high-risk operations know that leaders need to be able to communicate through plain words and direct action their vision for the culture and then sustain that culture - 'Defend the Village' as Jon writes. I agree. If you are a leader or an aspiring leader, pick up Jon's book and think about your organization. How are you shaping the culture in your organization? There is nothing more important that you can do as a leader to create and sustain a world class organization."

"In this extraordinarily important book, Jon Becker shows readers how to intentionally build a culture that reaches the highest performance. Culture is the organizational operating system and Becker entertains while he shows leaders how to execute at an elite level. A must read."

"Jon offers a forward-thinking perspective by examining the connections between corporate culture and the culture of elite units. His analysis highlights a powerful and often overlooked principle: effective leadership depends on the trust placed in those operating on the ground.

What stands out most is the responsibility leaders must assume—not only in empowering their teams with autonomy, but in fully owning the decisions those teams make, regardless of the outcome. True leadership is not about controlling every action; it is about creating the conditions in which skilled professionals can act decisively, while ensuring that accountability ultimately rests at the top.

During the operation conducted at the Bataclan, one of the decisive factors that enabled us to free all the hostages was the freedom of maneuver we were granted. That operational latitude allowed teams on the ground to adapt rapidly, make critical decisions in real time, and respond effectively to an evolving threat environment.

The lesson extends beyond elite units. Whether in crisis response or corporate strategy, organizations that cultivate trust, clarity of intent, and freedom of execution are better positioned to succeed in complex, high-stakes environments."

— JAY
Team Leader, BRI Paris

"In *Culture First*, lifelong scholar of law enforcement Jon Becker shows us that intellectual curiosity is the foundation of innovation and organizational success: necessary, but not sufficient, for winning decision cycling.

Broken into nine chapters— nine lessons, nine tightly-focused analyses of military and police tactics and operations — this book pulls us into the successes and failures of those sworn to protect and defend us all. His observations on culture come from his unique position: as a civilian with decades of daily experience in and around these communities, he stands apart from these elite teams but can give us a deep and thoughtful understanding of how these people work, and how they think. It is culture, in the end, that makes an organization succeed or fail. Becker's lessons are timely, and timeless. A must-read!"

— STANTON COERR, USMC (RET.)
Author: Rough Men Stand Ready,
Rubicon: The Poetry of War, *and* Undertow

"I have read a lot of leadership books over the years. Most diagnose culture from a distance. Jon Becker spent four decades inside it, while embedded with the world's most elite teams who don't have the luxury of getting culture wrong.

I watched *Culture First* be written by a man I've come to respect deeply. Jon joined me on Episode 103 of The Coffee and Change Podcast to share what those decades had taught him, and what stayed with me was how little he needed theory to make his point. He'd lived it. What he witnessed, and what he distills into actionable practices in his book, elevates culture from where it often gets placed by organizations, as a background condition. Instead, Jon reminds us that it's the work. And the cornerstone to success.

In my own work helping organizations navigate change, culture is consistently the thing that either accelerates or stops everything else. Becker names that dynamic with precision, highlighting those cultures leaders inherited and never examined. But he doesn't stop at naming the problem. He then hands you the tools to change it, and ultimately helps save lives. Whether you lead five people or five thousand, this book will make you examine what you've inherited and what you owe the people around you. As you read, you will find that the margin notes will start accumulating fast, and that is the sign of a great storyteller. Excited to share this book far and wide."

— BILL KIRST

Podcast Host and Change Leader

"In high-risk environments, culture isn't a slogan - it's what determines outcomes. Jon Becker understands that elite performance is built intentionally through standards, accountability, and leadership that puts the team first. *Culture First* captures the principles I've seen separate average teams from exceptional ones. This book translates hard-earned lessons from elite units into practical guidance for leaders in any arena."

— JORDAN MACWILLIAMS, RCMP-ERT

"I loved this book. A must read for leaders of all stripes with indispensable lessons for our challenging times."

"*Culture First* is a leadership book that manages to be both comprehensive and fundamental at the same time. It covers enormous ground without ever drifting into abstraction or unnecessary complexity. One of its greatest strengths is the total absence of jargon or over-engineering: just clear steps, thoughtful guidance, and lessons that translate into practical, immediately usable action.

Jon has always had a remarkable ability to look across industries, from SWAT teams to Fortune 500 companies, from elite military units to tech startups, and extract what actually matters. In this book, he pulls together the most valuable lessons about leadership and the deeper cultural forces that shape how organizations perform, reducing them to their essential ingredients and building them back into something cohesive, coherent, and deeply useful. It's a rare synthesis: versatile enough to apply anywhere, concrete enough to implement tomorrow, and fulfilling in a way only the simplest, truest ideas ever are.

And part of why it lands so well is because of who Jon is. His own internal culture - the way he leads, behaves, and treats people - shows up on every page. He embodies the qualities we all hope to see in those writing about leadership: humility without insecurity or defensiveness, generosity without ego, and a calm clarity in his presence that only comes with genuine wisdom earned over time. The book reflects not just his experience, but the values he lives by.

My hope is that any organization responsible for leading people operating under pressure - no matter what the pressure is - will read this book and apply it to their work environment, because the most meaningful thing a true leader can do is build and maintain an optimal environment for their people."

— DR. JENNIFER PROHASKA

Police Psychologist and Founder, Tactical Longevity